Bibliographic Information of the German National Library

The German National Library lists this publication in the German National Bibliography; detailed bibliographic data are available on the Internet at http://dnb.d-nb.de

Production and publishing
BoD - Books on Demand, Norderstedt

ISBN: 9783750421042

3   History of the Canary Islands

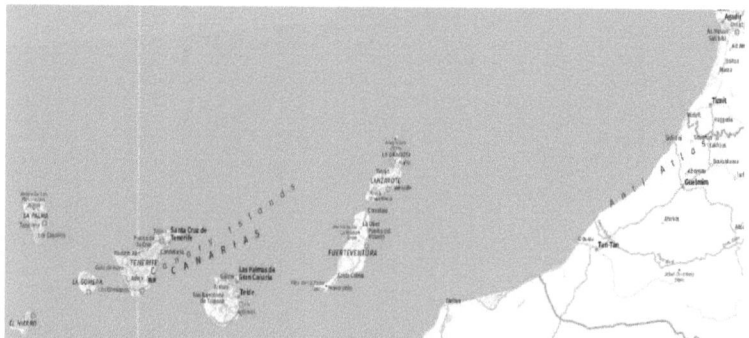

The archipelago consists of 8 islands: La Graciosa, Lanzarote, Fuerteventura, Gran Canaria, Tenerife, La Palma, La Gomera and El Hierro. They belong politically to Spain and geographically to Africa.
They are located 1200 km from the Spanish mainland and between 100 and 500 km west of Morocco. All islands are of volcanic origin, their age declines from east to west.
Millions of years ago enormous masses of magma pushed up through fracture lines of the earth's crust, exploded in violent volcanic eruptions and formed the islands with their basalt lava flows. In several eruption bursts of varying duration and intensity, they formed today's island profiles.
Fuerteventura with about 22 million years, Lanzarote and La Graciosa with 15.5 million years are the oldest islands of the archipelago. Gran Canaria was founded 14.5 million years ago, Tenerife 12 million years ago and La Gomera 11 million years ago. La Palma and El Hierro are the youngest Canary Islands with 2 and 1.2 million years respectively.
The aborigines descended from North African Berbers and developed different cultures on the individual islands, independently of each other. On Lanzarote they were called Majos, on Fuerteventura Majoreros, on Gran Canaria Canarios, on Tenerife Guanchen, on La Palma Benahoaritas, on La Gomera Gomeros and on El Hierro Bimbaches.
They lived at Stone Age level in caves and fed on collected plants, cultivated cereals and legumes, animal products, especially goats, and fish and shellfish near the coast.
The conquest and thus the subjugation of the Canary Islands took place between the years 1403 and 1496 by the Spanish crown.

1   Hint Cruises in a different way Compact   2
2   Imprint (German)   3
3   History of the Canary Islands   4
4   General Map Santa Cruz de Tenerife   5
5   Welcome to the capital Santa Cruz de Tenerife!   6
6   General Map Plaza Weyler, Plaza de Los Patos, Parque García Sanabria   14
7   General map Auditorio de Tenerife, Parque Marítimo Manrique, Cien Caras del Auditorio, Castillo de San Juan, Casa de la Pólvera and Palmetum   17
8   General Map Puerto del Rosario Fuerteventura   20
9   Welcome to the capital Puerto del Rosario of Fuerteventura!   21
10   General Map Las Palmas de Gran Canaria Centre   24
11   Welcome to the capital Las Palmas de Gran Canaria!   25
12   General Map Vegueta Gran Canaria   28
13   Old Town Tour - Vegueta Exploratory Tour   29
14   General Map Arrecife Lanzarote   38
15   Welcome to the capital Arrecife on Lanzarote!   39
16   General Maps Santa Cruz de la Palma   44
17   Welcome to the capital Santa Cruz de La Palma!   46
18   General Map San Sebastián de La Gomera   56
19   Welcome to the capital San Sebastián de La Gomera!   57
20   General Information Canaries   62
21   Index   66

1   Hint Cruises in a different way Compact

By Andrea Müller

Andrea Müller, Calle Las Cuevas, 91 - A2
E- 35542 Punta Mujeres, province of Las Palmas, Lanzarote
Web: www.fuerteventura-mal-anders.de
mailto:ebook@lfuerteventura-mal-anders.de

© 2019/2020 Andrea Müller, cover design, pictures: Andrea Müller
Map material mapz.com - Map Data OpenStreetMap ODbL
Number of pages Print variant: 72 pages
Number of images: 0 images 11 maps

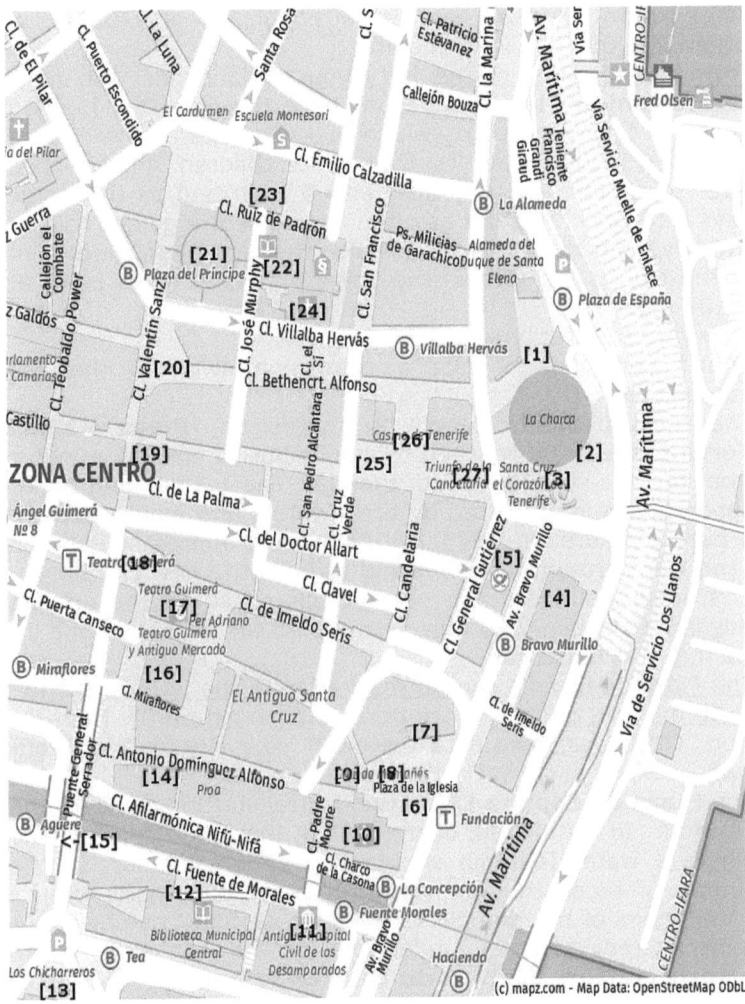

Space for your own notes🖉... ...

5   Welcome to the capital Santa Cruz de Tenerife!

You have now anchored in the port on the largest island with 2034 sq km. Tenerife has a total population of 920,000, of whom 203,000 live in the capital. From the terminal of the jetty you directly meet the main road **Avenida Marítima**. From here the Hop-On- Hop-Off buses of City View start, which you can take at the current price of € 22,00 for adults, € 11,00 for children. An attractive offer to explore the city also with a train and as the name says it to get in and out as often as you like. A guided tour of the city from the Plaza de España, the central starting point of the city, is included in the ticket price and takes place at 12.00 noon.
ⓘ www.tenerifecityview.com
Would you like to take a refreshing swim in the sea immediately?
The most beautiful beach on the island, **Playa de las Teresitas**, can be reached by public bus in only 15 minutes from the bus stop in front of the pier. The 1.3 km long bright sandy beach is protected by breakwaters and makes bathing a pure pleasure. In 1973, 100,000 cubic metres of Saharan sand were brought to the island to build the new city beach. Chargeable loungers and beach stalls round off the offer. 🚌 Bus line 910, every 20 min. from 05.10 am at 30, 50 and 10 each,ⓘ www.titsa.com
The Plaza de España can be reached from the jetty to the left in 10 minutes on foot. From here you can get on the Hop- On Hop- Off buses, take a taxi or start your city walk on your own.
The **Plaza de España [1]** is the central starting point for the city tour. In the middle of the square there is a circular lake where a water fountain shoots up every half hour. In the course of reconstruction works in July 2006, parts of the foundations of the demolished Castillo de San Cristóbal were rediscovered, so that under the square the **Centro de Interpretación Castillo de San Cristóbal [2]** was built, where the remains can be viewed. Access is from the side of the lake in the direction of the sea. The Castillo was built in 1577, had a size of 50 x 53 meters, 4 corner towers and 8.3 m high defensive walls inland. Equipped with cannons and a permanent crew of 30-40 artillerymen, it played an important role in the defence of the port during the English attacks of the 17th and 18th centuries by Blake, Jennings and Nelson. Legend has it that a 16 caliber cannon called El Tigre was

fired near the Castillo at the dawn of 25.07.1797, with which the right forearm of Admiral Nelson was shot down. The original cannon, which since then has stood as a symbol of the victory over the mighty English Armada, was built and exhibited on a replica carriage.☉ Mon-Sat 10:00-18:00, Sun closed, 🎟 free admission.

The course of the foundation walls of the Castillo at that time is marked with a black mark in the lake towards the town.

On the side is the **Monumento a los Caídos [3]** from 1947, dedicated to the victims of the civil war in Santa Cruz. It consists of a 25m high cruciform tower with a platform that is no longer accessible. Above the stroke "Tenerife en honor a todos los que dieron su vida por España" - Tenerife, in honour of all those who gave their lives for Spain - the sculpture holding a fallen man in its arms is a symbol for the fatherland. Among them, the winged woman embodies victory. The relief depictions on the sides depict struggle and peace. In front of the monument there are 2 oversized soldiers leaning on their swords. They symbolize civic and military values.

On the left, behind the monument, there is the **Cabildo de Tenerife [4]**, the building of the island administration, dating from 1940, which can be recognised by its high tower.

To the right is the main post office, the **Edificio de Correos y Telegrafos [5]**, from 1946. Between the buildings, the street Calle de Bravo Murillo continues along the tramway crossing the railway tracks - Attention! - to the small cobbled **Plaza de la Iglesia [6]**. On the right side, behind the two large Indian laurel trees, there were 4 tobacco factories. One of them, the Fabrica de Tabacos **La Tinerfeña [7]** tobacco factory, which can be recognized by the inscription on the houses, was founded in 1880 by Manuel Herrera and already used advanced technology to produce 80,000 cigarettes per hour.

Next to the plaza there is a small garden fenced in with bars, at the end of which stands a large marble cross, the **Cruz de Montañés [8]**. It was founded in 1759 by Captain Bartolomé Antonio Méndez Montañés and dignifiedly symbolizes the name of the city (Santa Cruz = Holy Cross).

In the building block behind it is the house of the Carta family, **Casa de Carta** (No. 6) **[9]** from the time of the bourgeoisie. From the typical Canarian wooden balcony one could see all the way to the harbour.

Special attention should be paid to the church **Iglesia de la Concepción [10]** on the left side. It was consecrated in 1502 and is the oldest church in the city. Built in a Canarian-Moorish style, its appearance was greatly altered after a fire in 1652. The six-storey tower with a bell tower made of red volcanic stone is striking. Access is via Calle Padre Moore at the rear. The surrounding, typically Canarian wooden balcony above the entrance portal is unique on the islands. The interior of the five-aisled church is pompously designed. Next to the altar is the large original wooden cross with silver fittings, which the Spaniard Alonso Fernández de Lugo is said to have rammed into the ground here in 1496 after the conquest of the island. ✪daily 9-20 o'clock

Here you can decide whether you would like to visit the following points additionally. The tour continues again from the church.

On the left over the bridge Puente de El Cabo you directly reach the Museum of Nature and Archaeology, the **Museo de la Naturaleza y Arqueología- MUNA [11]**, which is housed in a former hospital. In two permanent exhibitions, the geological, climatic and biological conditions of the Canary Islands are shown on the one hand, and the history of the Canary Islands native population is presented with archaeological finds on the other. Very interesting are tools, cult objects, petroglyphs as well as the mummies and mummy remains found on the island. ✪ Di- Sa 9-20, So- Mo 10-17 Uhr, 24./25./31.12, 01/06.01 and carnival Tuesday closed, ▲admission free

The Tenerife Espacio de las Artes- TEA [12] to the right is the contemporary art and culture centre of the city. The long glass exposed concrete building was designed by the Swiss architects Herzog& de Meuren. Permanent and temporary exhibitions take place on more than 20,000 sqm. It is the seat of the Óscar Domínguez Institute, which permanently displays the works of the surrealist painter of the same name, born in Tenerife. It is also home to the Photography Centre, which aims to disseminate and preserve the photographic culture of the island and other countries. The complex is completed by the Central Library and a large souvenir shop with certified handicrafts, accessible from the outside via the Plaza de La Sierra. ✪ Di- Sun 10-20 o'clock, ▲ adults €7,00, seniors €5,00, children under 12 years and students up to 26 years free (ID required)

Opposite the souvenir shop is the **Mercado de Nuestra Señora de África [13]**, popularly known as La Recova. It is the shopping address for a wide variety of foodstuffs. The old pink building is in neoclassical style and was inaugurated in 1944. A lively hustle and bustle takes place at the stands, which drape themselves around a patio down to the basement. daily ☉7-14 o'clock. On the left side in front of the entrance is a sculpture of a fishing boat pushed into the sea by two men. It's a tribute to the Chicharreos. According to tradition, this name dates back to the 16th century and refers to the origins of the town as a small coastal town where fishing was the main source of income. To the left of the market hall is the **Rambla Azul** with blue pavilions and other shopping facilities under a tree-lined avenue.

Back to Iglesia de la Concepción: The rows of buildings on the left of the church in Calle Antonio Domínguez Alfonso were originally owned by poor fishermen who painted their houses in the same colours as their boats to make them easier to recognise. In the meantime the carnival associations of the island are located here (house no. 7, 13 and 15).

A little further up the street, at the corner of Callejón del Miedo, next to house number 29, behind three large Indian laurel trees is the house of terror, the **Casa del Miedo [14]**, where the carnival association Asociación Cultural Mamel´s is located. According to legend, two brothers lived here. Since one of them was constantly drunk and staggering running home, the children made fun of him. In the evening he put two candles and a skull in the window to scare the children. Since then peace returned...

Optionally there is the Carnival Museum, the **Casa de Carnaval [15]**, signposted up the road, under the bridge through, left. On more than 1000 sqm you will learn everything about the colourful carnival hustle and bustle in the capital, which is the second largest in the world after Rio de Janeiro. The heart of the permanent and temporary exhibition is the pompous and award-winning costume of the Carnival Queen. ☉daily 9-19 am, ♦free admission, ⌂ Calle Aguere, 17

The road back, then left the Calzada la Noria high, was over corner the first department store of the city, where today the clothing shop **Confecciones BBB-** Buenas, Bonitas, Baratas- clothing BBB- good, beautiful and cheap, is located.

To the left, on the street Calle Santo Domingo you come to the square **Isla de la Madera**. On the left is the cultural centre **Centro de Arte La Recova [16]**. The temporary exhibitions are housed in an ancient market hall dating from 1851. The entrance is on the opposite side. ☉ Tue-Sat 11-13/ 17-20, Sun+ holidays 11-14 h, ⚊ free admission
The bronze sculpture of the local poet and playwright Ángel Guimerà y Jorge (1845-1924), who gave his name to the **Teatro Guimerà [17]** on the right, stands in the middle between the buildings. It was built on the site of the demolished monastery of Santo Domingo according to the plans of the first provincial architect Manuel de Oràa and inaugurated in 1851. Over the centuries it has been modernized several times and was the seat of the symphony orchestra until the inauguration of the auditorium. On the side is the large sculpture of a **theatre mask**, whose laughing mouth on the front stands for the comedy, and sad mouth on the back for the tragedy.
The itinerary continues to the right of the sculpture, across the tram tracks, up Calle Imeldo Seris to the left. You will find the small **Plaza Santo Domingo [18]** with an old Indian laurel tree, a pretty flower bed and the fountain Fuente de Santo Domingo from the 19th century. The lateral **bronze sculpture** of a water bearer is intended to remind us of the women who once drew water here to sell it to wealthy citizens.
On the opposite side of the street is the **Gobierno de Canarias**, the island government building with a square tower clock above the entrance portal, which is unique in the Canary Islands.
The lively shopping street Calle Valentín Sanz begins to the right of the square. (Optionally, from here you can turn left onto the Puente Serrador bridge, which leads to the Mercado de Nuestra Señora de África in about 5 minutes). After approx. 50 m you will see the Mango clothing store on your right, with **tiled billboards [19]** on its façade. The advertisements for the bazaar, Perfumeria and Emulsion Scott are exemplary for all the billboards that were once placed throughout the city centre as they can be seen here.
Continuing straight on, crossing the main shopping street Calle del Castillo, you come to the **Plaza del Chicharro [20]** with the bronze sculpture El Chicharro, a fish on a wave, which is supposed to remind of the typical fish of the island which was caught and sold in Santa Cruz at that time.

Behind it stands a particularly beautiful specimen of a dragon tree.

Continue up the road and you will see **Plaza Principe de Asturias [21]** on your right, a 6000 square metre park with a central pavilion. At the end of the 17th century, the Franciscan monastery of San Pedro de Alcántara was founded in Santa Cruz and expropriated by Spain in 1820. To the west of the monastery was the vegetable garden. In order to get a better access to the town hall, which was housed in the monastery building, a street was built between the former monastery and the monastery garden. After the town council acquired the land in 1857, the architect Manuel de Oráa drew up the plans for a park. He filled the area to the level of the western square and built walls and stairs. The park was named after the Spanish heir to the throne who was born on 28.11.1857, the later Alfonso XII. In 1866 Indian laurel trees were imported from Cuba for the design of the park, and in 1868 two marble sculptures representing summer and spring were erected on the west side, now the entrance. In front of the pavilion, which was erected in 1930, stands on the left the **sculpture of Enrique González Bethencourt**, the founder and leader of the carnival group Ni Fú Ni Fá, the father of the Tenerife carnival. From here his family watched him perform in the pavilion. Already in Franco times, when carnival activities were forbidden, he was the most important carnivalist, who is also shown on a photo in the Casa de Carnaval.

On the terrace of Kiosco El Principe you can take a breather between the locals with a view of the green park. Then you walk from here through the park.

At the eastern end, stairs lead directly to the **Museo Municipal de Bellas Artes [22]**, the City Museum of Fine Arts. The reddish-brown building with sandstone columns and busts of prominent city fathers on the upper floor of the facade was built in classicist style and redesigned several times. The museum was founded in 1840. At that time, the city council decided to preserve the flags left behind by the English attack on Santa Cruz in 1797 under the command of Admiral Nelson. Currently, various collections of Dutch and Canarian painters from the 16th to 19th centuries are exhibited in the rooms. ☻ Di- Sun 10-14 ♪ Admission free ⌂ Calle José Murphy, 12

To the left of the museum is the magnificent turquoise-yellow building of the **Círculo de Amistad XII de Enero [23]**,

built between 1904 and 1934 and accessible only to club members. ⌂ Calle Ruíz Padrón, 12
To the right of the museum, house no. 10, is the **Parish Office** of **Parroquia San Francisco**, in house no. 8 is the entrance to the **Convent of San Pedro de Alcantara Franciscanos**, but both are inaccessible.

Go left down Calle Villalba Hervas and you will immediately come to the side entrance of the church of **Iglesia de San Francisco [24]**, which was the temple of the old monastery founded by the Franciscans around 1680. Expansion and reform work was carried out in the 17th and 18th centuries. The originally single-nave temple was extended to three and separated by semicircular arches resting on red tuff columns. The three large gilded altar walls are magnificent. The main altar was carved in 1733 and gilded between 1736 and 1739. It is one of the most beautiful and interesting of the Canary Islands, as it is exceptionally planty and pictorial. The wooden ceilings are in Mudejar style and the baroque altarpieces and murals date from the 18th century. ◐ 8:13-17:30-20 hours. If the side entrance is closed, go further down the building facade and you will come across the corner of the main Baroque portal of the church. The **Tribunal de Justicia**, the court building of the capital, joins here.

Now turn into Calle San Francisco on the opposite side of the street and after the crossroad you will come to the large **Plaza La Candelaria [25]**. At the beginning of the 16th century, the entire area of the present square was used for militia exercises, so that it was called Plaza de las Armas. In 1579, the construction of the Castillo San Cristóbal separated the square from the sea, and other buildings were erected. Due to the increase in importance of the port, which was provided with a pier in front of the Castillo, the square was given the name Plaza del Castillo and became the economic centre of Santa Cruz. With the demolition of the Castillo in 1929, the square was reopened to the sea, but lost its importance due to the new layout and development of the adjacent Plaza de España and was completely redesigned into a pedestrian zone in 2008. In the upper part of the square you come directly to a small **fountain with a bowl**, which was built in 1706. Here was one of the end points of the drinking water supply of the city and the port, which brought the water from the northern Anaga mountains via a 12 km long canal.

On the left side, between the clothing store Zara and the Hotel Plaza, stands the **Palacio de Carta [26]**. The historically important building was erected by one of the richest and most influential families on the island between 1721 and 1752 and has been a listed building since 1947. You have seen a simpler residential house of the Carta family on your tour next to the church Iglesia de la Concepción. The Palacio is currently being restored by the island government and will be open to the public in the future.

Walk down the pedestrian zone towards the sea and you will see the **Casino de Santa Cruz de Tenerife**, built in 1935 and listed since 2006, on the left façade of the building. This is not a public casino, but a private association for the promotion of culture and leisure activities, which is only accessible to members.

Now it's time for the end of the city tour. On the left, above the lake, you can see the monument **El Triunfo de La Candelaria [27]**, erected in honour of the island's patron saint, the Virgen de La Candelaria. The top of the obelisk is crowned by a statue of the Virgin Mary. The figures standing at the corners of the pedestal represent the four indigenous princes of the island - the Menceys - from the principalities of Icod, Daute, Abona and Adeje.

Space for your own notes✐ ... ...

6 General Map Plaza Weyler, Plaza de Los Patos, Parque García Sanabria

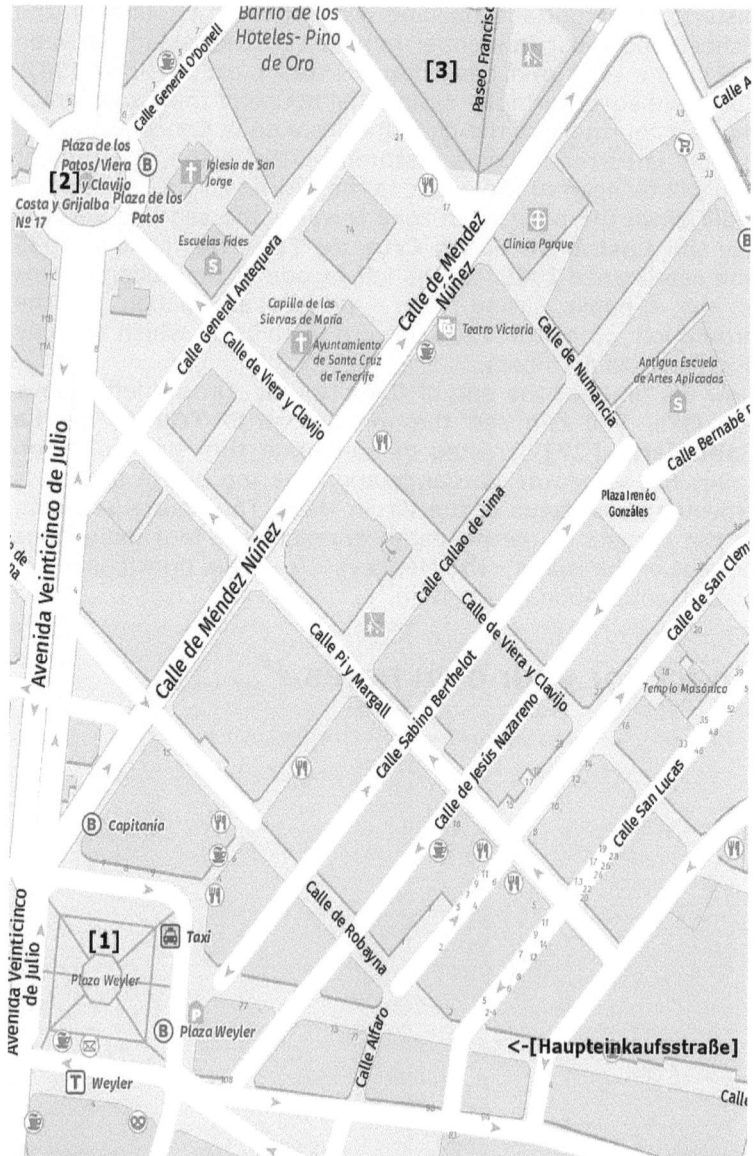

ATTENTION: Haupteinkaufsstraße = main shopping street

Do you just want to relax in the three beautiful parks of Santa Cruz? You have to come here, it is a little further on foot, but will be started on the Hop- On Hopp- Off Tour. Alternatively, the cost of a taxi from the boat or from the Plaza de España is a maximum of € 10.00 per leg.

Plaza Weyler [1]

A popular meeting place for the locals is **Plaza Weyler**, which is located at the end of the main shopping street Calle del Castillo. It was designed as a forecourt for the General Quarter with the Palacio de la Capitanía General de Canarias, which is located above the square. In particular, the square goes back to the Spanish General Valeriano Weyler, the General Captain of the Canary Islands. The white, almost 6 m high marble fountain from the year 1899 stands in the centre. At the corners of the fountain children sit with dolphins in their hands, from whose mouths water runs into the shells underneath.

Plaza de los Patos [2]

Plaza de 25 de Julio is located at the crossroads of Avenida 25 de Julio and Calle Viera y Clavijo, and refers in particular to the attack of the English on Santa Cruz on 25 July 1797, popularly known as **Plaza de los Patos**, a duck square. It captivates by a large colorfully tiled fountain with water-spouting green ceramic frogs. The middle is adorned with the sculpture of a turtle, on whose shell sits a water-spouting bird. It is controversial whether this is a duck or a goose. The course is completed by 26 colourfully tiled benches.

Originally, there was no square at this intersection, but the erection of a equestrian monument for General Leopoldo O`Donnell from Santa Cruz was planned. As the donations for the monument were not sufficient, a small fountain was initially erected in 1909. When the square was redesigned in 1913, a pond was created on which ducks sometimes swam, which led to its current name. In the following years beds were planted and Indian laurel trees were planted. Inspired by the Latin American exhibition in Seville in 1930, the city council decided to redesign the square in the Sevillian style and to install a copy of the Fuente de las Ranas - the Frog Fountain - from the Maria Luisa Park in Seville, as well as benches with ceramic tiles. The names of the business sponsors were embedded in the front of the benches.

Parque García Sanabria [3]
It is the largest urban park in the Canary Islands with an area of 6.7 hectares and was declared a cultural monument in 2006. It was named after the mayor of the same name, who approved the building and carried out the work between 1924 and 1926 thanks to cash donations and natural produce in the form of plant cuttings. In addition to a lush flora of endemic and exotic plants, you will encounter memorial and contemporary sculptures. Of particular note is the **Monumento a Santiago García Sanabiria**, located in the centre of the park.

The monument is a large fountain with different jets of water and an obelisk in which several sculptures carved in stone stand. The most important is the naked woman who symbolizes fertility.

Also worth seeing is the large flower clock, the **Roloj de Flores**, which is located at the entrance of the street Calle Doctor José Navieras. It is permanently planted with fresh, colourful flowers, has a Swiss Favag movement and was donated by the Danish Consul Larsen in 1958.

Space for your own notes✎ ... ...

7 General map Auditorio de Tenerife, Parque Marítimo Manrique, Cien Caras del Auditorio, Castillo de San Juan, Casa de la Pólvera and Palmetum

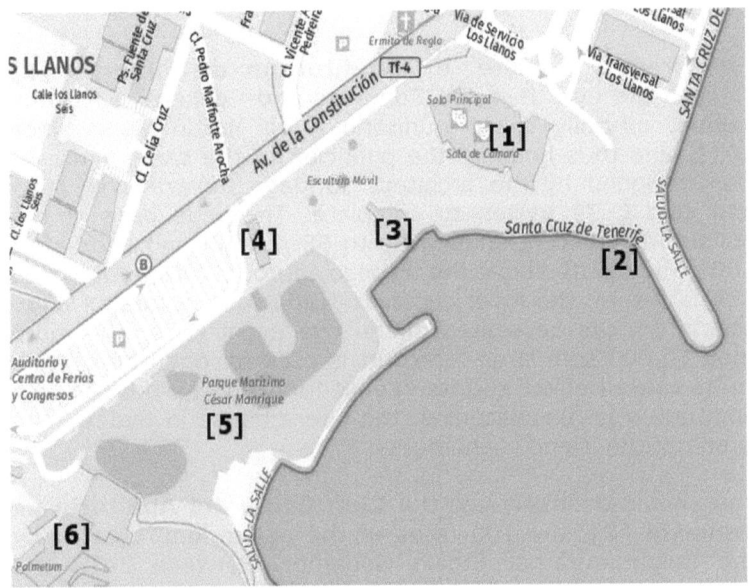

Space for your own notes✐... ...

At the end of the capital there are **6 further attractions** to visit, for which it is recommended to take a taxi from the Plaza de España. Alternatively, from the Plaza de España, follow the main road Avenida Marítima along the sea. After 1.5 km and approx. 20 minutes on foot you can reach the sights.

Even from a distance, the **Auditorium de Tenerife [1]** catches the eye. It is the Congress and Concert Hall of the capital, officially called Auditorio Adán Martín Menis since 2011, and thus honours the politician of the same name. It was designed by the architect Santiago Calatrava in 1989 and cost € 72 million to complete. The wide base of the building is crescent-shaped up to 58 m high and ends after 100 m in a peak above the trapezoidal roof. With a total area of 6,300 sqm, the foyer occupies 1,200 sqm. A total of 2086 spectators can be seated in the two event halls. The more than 16,000 sqm large forecourt is used for open-air events. In its overall effect and its exposed location by the sea, the auditorium is reminiscent of the opera house in Sydney and is one of the island's landmarks.

You should definitely see the **Cien Caras del Auditorio de Tenerife [2]**, the 100 faces of the auditorium, created by the Bulgarian artist Stoiko Gagamor. Between 2010 and 2011, small works of art in the form of painted portraits of musicians were created on the black natural stones and concrete blocks at the pier on the right side of the auditorium to the adjoining Castillo San Juan between 2010 and 2011. The artist started with the pictures of the auditorium architect Santiago Calatrava and the singer Luciano Pavarotti and added 98 more within 8 months. These include Elvis Presley, Beethoven, Mozart and Abba.

To the right is the **Castillo de San Juan [3]**. The fortress was built in 1644 and was the second most important defensive structure on the city's coast, after the Castillo de San Cristóbal. The round building was made of black basalt stones, has a diameter of 30 m, a height of 8 m and 2.5 m thick walls. With the open forecourt and balustrades for loopholes it offered space for 5 artillery guns. The wooden drawbridge led up a stone staircase to 2 watchtowers. The Castillo housed a supervisor, numerous soldiers and had a gunpowder store. It is the best preserved fortress in Tenerife, but it is currently inaccessible to visitors.

Immediately next door is the **Casa de la Pólvera [4]**, the house of gunpowder, built in 1756. In the 10 m wide and 30 m long building with barrel vault, up to 1.5 tons of gunpowder were stored dry, despite being close to the sea. To prevent the powder chamber from being seen and bombed from the sea by enemy ships, a high wall was erected around the building in 1779, which no longer exists. Only the memorial stone on the front left side gives an impression of the original course of the wall.
If you now go up the stairs, you will reach the next attraction. The **Parque Marítimo César Manrique [5]** is one of Santa Cruz's hotspots, with over 22,000 square metres. In the strandless and unattractive harbour area, the famous Lanzarote artist César Manrique created a unique oasis of well-being that is still unique today. The spacious seawater pools with central islands made of natural lava stones occupy almost half of the area. This year-round resort is a pure and refreshing bathing experience for young and old, complemented by restaurants and a small beach by the sea. ☼ 10-18 ♨ 2,50 €, children under 2 years free of charge, couches 2,50 € p.p., parasol 3,00 €, more ①www.parquemaritimosantacruz.es
To get to the last sight you turn right, along the parking lot, to a fantastic paradise on the outskirts of the big city. The **Palmetum [6]** is a 12-hectare botanical garden that was created on a former waste dump in the capital.

The largest palm collection in Europe grows here. Along the route you can admire beautiful vantage points, small streams, lakes and waterfalls. ☼daily 10-18 h♨ 6.00 €, children up to 11 years free of charge, ①for the approx. 1.5 h tour you can buy a map with 21 special points and explanations of the palm species at the cash desk for 0.50 €, or download the app with all information free of charge to your smartphone. ⌂ Avenida de la Constitución, 5, ①www.palmetumtenerife.es

Space for your own notes✐... ...

8 General Map Puerto del Rosario Fuerteventura

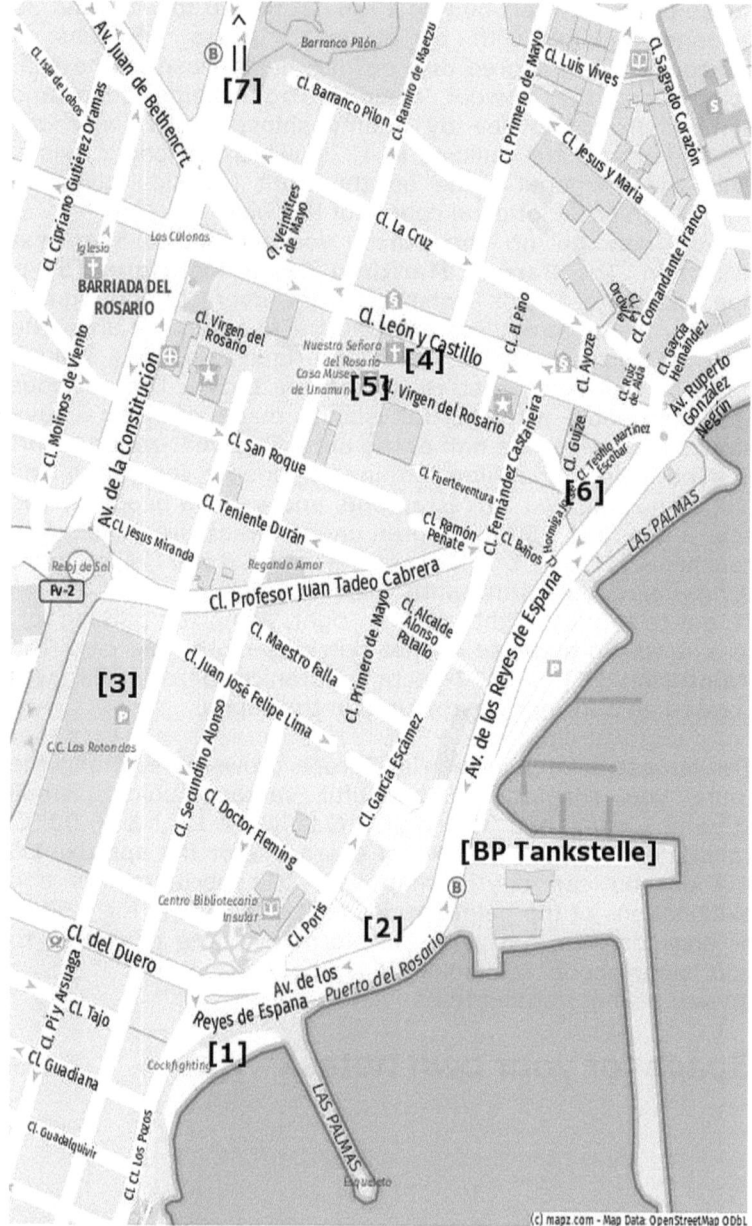

ATTENTION: BP Tankstelle = BP Petrol Station

9 Welcome to the capital Puerto del Rosario of Fuerteventura!

You have now anchored in the port on the 2nd largest island with 1660 sqkm. Fuerteventura has a total population of 115,000, of whom 36,000 live in the capital. Above the mooring is the centre of the capital Fuerteventura. The BP petrol station, along which the main road Avenida Reyes de España runs, serves as a landmark.

If you follow the promenade to the left, you will arrive directly at the well-kept, fine sandy city beach **Playa Chica [1]**.

To get to the **city centre,** cross the crosswalk at the BP petrol station and turn left. After the 2nd building on the right you will come to a small square **[2]** above the stairs leading up to the city centre Centro Ciudad. At the end you will pass Calle García Escámez and automatically arrive at Calle Dr. Flemming. Now there are 2 options to choose from: if you continue along the street, you will end up at the largest shopping centre in Fuerteventura, the **Centro Comercial Las Rotondas [3]**.☉ Mo Sat 10 - 20 o'clock, Sun closed① All information to the current mark shops under: www.lasrotondascentrocomercial.com

If you take the first street to the right, Calle Primero Mayo begins, which was the pulsating artery of the capital before the opening of the shopping centre. Nearly all shops were closed and moved to the new center, so that in the cruise free time one meets an almost deserted pedestrian zone, in which only a few cafes are still open.

Shortly before the end of the Avenida, at the confluence of Calle Virgen del Rosario, there is the **Cabildo**, the town hall of the city, in front of which there is a souvenir pavilion with typical souvenirs of the island.☉ Mon-Fri 10.15- 13.30, 17.30- 20 o'clock

Behind it is the parish church of **Nuestra Señora del Rosario [4]**. It was built in 1812 and was the first religious building in the centre of the island. It was a small house of prayer dedicated to the Virgin El Rosario. In the years 1824-1835 the central bell tower was added, which is today integrated into the east façade. The wrought-iron, ornate lattices on the main portal are conspicuous. In the middle of the high altar is the patron saint of the church with the Child Jesus on her arm.

The Casa Museo Unamuno museum [5] is located in the row of houses to the left of the church. The building was registered in 1877 in the land register of Puerto de Cabras, the original name of Puerto del Rosario. At that time it was a small guesthouse, called "Hotel Fuerteventura", where the Spanish writer Miguel de Unamuno lived on the island for 5 months during his exile. The museum is a testimony of the typical architecture of Canarian houses from that time.

⊙daily 9-14 am, ♨admission free, ⓪additional information: Miguel de Unamuno was professor and rector of the Spanish University in Salamanca. On 12 March 1924 he was banished to Fuerteventura by the then head of state because of critical statements against the regime. He lived 5 months on the island in exile, made me friends with the inhabitants and wrote down his impressions about Fuerteventura, which were published in daily newspapers in Madrid, Buenos Aires and Gran Canaria. He then voluntarily fled to France to take up his fight outside Spain against the dictatorship. On his 100th birthday, the island government erected a monument to him on the Montaña Quemada, not far from the village of Tindaya.

In the city you can visit 2 weekly food markets:

Mercado Municipal [6]: If you go to the end of Calle Primero de Mayo, you come to Calle Léon y Catillo, which you follow to the right in the direction of the sea. Before the roundabout, turn right into Calle Teófilo Martínez Escobar and follow the road until you see the Mercado Municipal on your left. The traders offer a selection of fruit, vegetables, meat, fish and goat cheese. ⊙ Mon-Fri 7-13 ⓪Visit this small market with friendly sellers while it is still possible. Due to a small number of visitors, it could be foreseeable that this small market hall will no longer exist permanently.

Mercado Agrario de Fuerteventura [7]: At the end of Calle de Primero Mayo, turn left into Calle Léon y Castillo,which you follow to the left. You come to a roundabout and the main road Avenida La Constitución, which you follow to the right. Before the 2nd roundabout which leads to the right into the Avenida Diego Miller, the building of the central bus station **Estación de Guagas** is located, with the market in the upper floor. Homemade products and regional food are offered. ⊙ Sat 8-14 o'clock

⓪This might interest you, too: Strolling along the beach promenade you will encounter many sculptures by local artists. In the city centre you can see the graffiti art on old residential buildings. In January 2011, the planning office decided to have the dilapidated building facades of the capital embellished. After consultation with the owners, the Concurso de Arte Urbano de Puerto de Rosario, a competition for artistic design, was announced in 2015. Meanwhile more than 36 artists were allowed to realize their works on house walls. Due to positive feedback from islanders and tourists this project will be continued.

Space for your own notes✐... ...

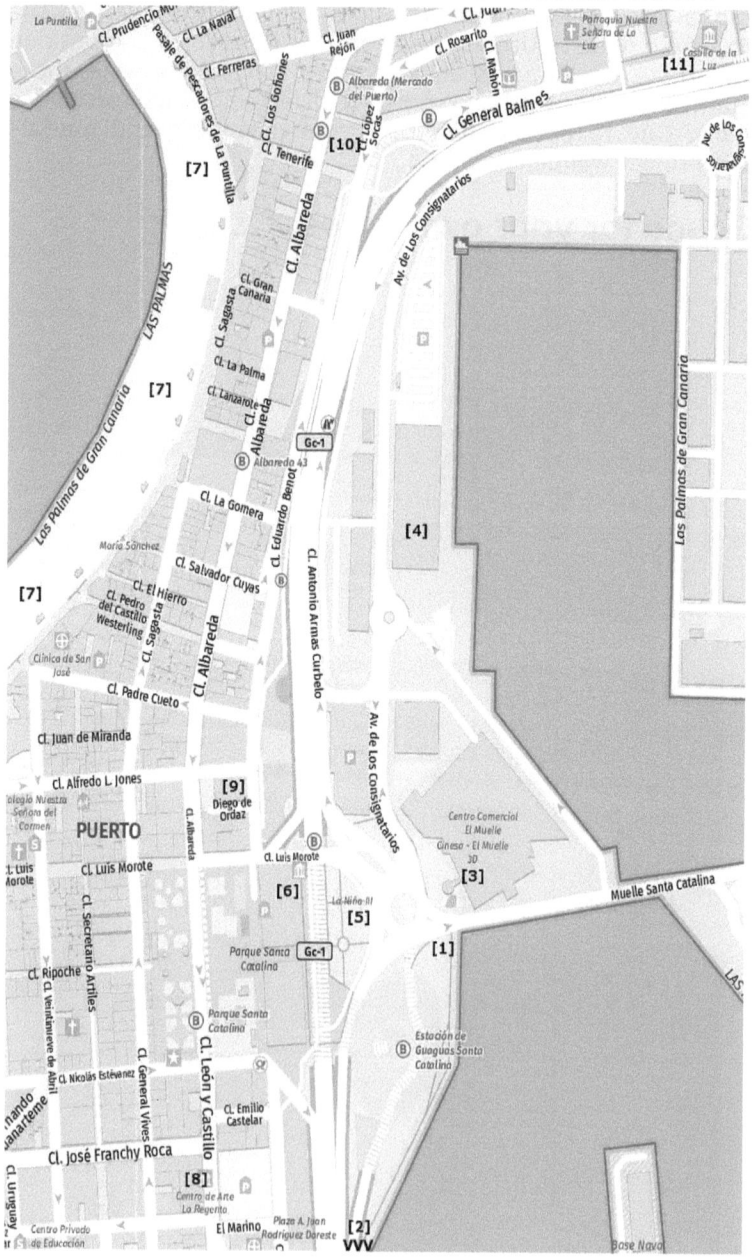

11 Welcome to the capital Las Palmas de Gran Canaria!

You have now anchored in the port on the 3rd largest island with 1560 sqkm. Gran Canaria has a total of 857,000 inhabitants, of whom 378,000 live in the capital. Enjoy your shore leave and profit from the many possibilities **Las Palmas** and the old town **La Vegueta** has to offer. Unfortunately, you have to decide whether you want to make the big city unsafe directly in Las Palmas and take a bath in the sea of the Atlantic Ocean, or rather explore the heart of the historic old town La Vegueta.

From the jetty, go up Muelle Santa Catalina towards the city. On the left side is the small box of the **tourist information [1]**, in front of which the Hop-On Hop- Off buses start.

Optionally you can go from here to **Playa de Las Alcaravaneras [2]**, which can be reached in 15 minutes on foot after approx. 1 km. After the city beach Playa de Las Canteras (10 min./ 850 m) Playa de Las Alcaravaneras is the second most visited beach of Las Palmas.

To get to the 550 m long light brown fine sandy beach, go left past the tourist information office and follow the footpath along the pier to the left along the main road Calle General Balmes, which becomes Calle León y Castillo and leads to the yacht club Real Club Náutico de Gran Canaria. Afterwards the beach starts with a beach view, free changing rooms, showers and toilets. The sheltered beach is especially suitable for children.

Opposite the tourist information is the large shopping centre, the **Centro Comercial El Muelle [3]**.⏀ All shops and restaurants under www.ccelmuelle.es◉ Mon-Sat 10- 22 o'clock, Sun. are opened only the restaurants starting from 12.00 o'clock.

To get to **Aquarium Poema del Mar [4]**, turn right in front of the shopping centre and follow the road. It is one of the most spectacular aquariums in the world and was opened in December 2017 on an area of 12,500 sqm. More than 350 exotic and native species can be seen. The main attraction is the huge aquarium with the largest rounded disc ever built. It weighs over 140 tons, is 35 m wide and has a capacity of 5.5 million litres.◉ Daily 9- 18 h ▲Adults: € 25,00, children under 4 years free, from 4 to 11 years € 17,50 ⌂ Muelle de Sanapú

To get to the <u>city centre,</u> cross the street to the right of the shopping centre and follow the street. On the left side you can see the sailing ship **La Carabela III [5]** embedded in the ground on a green area. It is a historical, true to original replica from 1992 and one of 3 ships with which Christopher Columbus embarked on his first voyage to discover the New World in 1492. The reconstruction was carried out by the Spanish captain Carlos Etayo Elizondo, who had this caravel built in Pontevedra in northern Spain after many years of study.

In honour of the 500-year-old discovery of America, the Carabela III of Huelva sailed with 13 crew members, 3 of them from Gran Canaria, first to Las Palmas. In order to faithfully recreate the sea voyage across the Atlantic, the island of La Gomera was also passed. The successful implementation has not yet been realized again.

After this trip, the ship was bought by the island government and the Fundación Mapfre Guanarteme and moored in the port of El Muelle Deportivo de Las Palmas. For his last trip the Carabela III went to Portugal to the EXPO 98 and back.

① By the way: Christopher Columbus set off for the New World with 3 ships, the Carabela III, which is called Niña 3, as well as the Santa Maria and the Carabela Pinta. Total ship length: 17.30 m, width: 4.12 m, height from keel to front: 1.73 m, unladen weight: 36.31 tons, average draught: 1.2 m, draught bow: 0.9 m, draught stern: 1.5 m

Behind it is the three-storey business and technology museum **Museo Elder [6]**. It is housed in a former hall for shipping goods from the 19th century and is one of the most important museums in the capital. A wide range of topics are offered, from mathematics to physics, art, biology and engineering. So you can try out sensory experiences such as flight simulator, planetarium, 3D cinema and other activities.☉ Daily 9-18 ♪€ 6.00, children under 6 free A ①free audio guide is offered for the smartphone (don't forget your headphones!). The ticket is valid all day, so you can enter and leave.

To the right of the Museum Elder, Calle Luis Marote leads directly to the city beach **Playa de las Canteras [7]** in approx. 10 minutes on foot.

One of the sights of Las Palmas is the more than 3 km long fine sandy city beach, which the inhabitants call the "bañera grande" - the big bathtub. Sunbathing and bathing is possible all year round, sunbeds and umbrellas are available for a fee. Along the long promenade countless restaurants invite you to stay.

As a beach alternative there are 2 further possibilities.

1st option: To the right of the museum, from Calle Luis Marote take the 1st street on the left into Calle Albareda, which leads through the Parque Santa Catalina with numerous cafés and bars. At the end of the park, the street changes to Calle Léon y Castillo, which you continue to follow until you reach the **La Regenta Museum [8]** on the right. In the building of a former tobacco factory, which was built at the beginning of the 20th century, there are temporary exhibitions of modern artists. ☻ Di- Fr 10- 14/ 17- 21Uhr, Sa 10-14 Uhr, Su, Mo, Fei closed ♨ Admission free ⌂ Calle León y Castillo, 427 ⓘCurrent exhibitions at www.laregenta.org

Option 2: Walk to the right of the museum from Calle Luis Marote to Calle Eduardo Benot and on the left you will find the striking **Hotel AC Gran Canaria [9]**. Built in the 1967's, the hotel is one of the most prominent points in the Parque Santa Catalina area. The floor plan is a hexagon with 16 balconies each on 26 floors. On the 23rd floor there is a public café with a fantastic view over the capital. ♨ Admission free ⌂ Calle Eduardo Benot 3,5 ⓘFrom the hotel entrance you have direct access to the lift.

To taste authentic tapas in a market hall, follow the road and after 650 m you will reach the **Mercado del Puerto [10]**. It is the market hall of the harbour, where 28 stands offer meat, fish, cheese, fruit and vegetables, as well as tapas and pinchos typical of the island.☻ Daily from 7.30- 00.00 ⌂ Calle Albareda, 76

After the market hall, turn right into Calle Poeta Agustin Millares Sall, which becomes Plaza Nuestra Señora de la Luz. You follow the road and come to a fenced park with the **Castillo de la Luz [11]**. The Castillo was the first port fortress built in the 16th century and successfully protected Las Palmas from pirate attacks. In 1969 the castle was rebuilt and declared a cultural asset. The museum was inaugurated in 2014 by King Felipe of Spain and his wife Letizia. Since 2015, the Fundación de Arte y Pensamiento, the foundation and exhibition of the artist Martín Chirino, has been located in the building. ☻ Tue-Sun 10-19♨ € 4,00 ⌂ Calle Juan Rejón s/n

12 General Map Vegueta Gran Canaria

13 Old Town Tour - Vegueta Exploratory Tour

When the Spanish conqueror Juan Rejón anchored on 24.06.1478 with a reign of 600 soldiers on the coast off La Isleta, he met only volcanic rock and sand dunes, so that he moved with his army further south. At the river Barranco de Guiniguada at that time, which nowadays only carries water after heavy rain, the conqueror founded a settlement under palm trees after the subjugation of the natives, which led to the original naming of the capital Ciudad Real de Las Palmas - city of palm trees. Las Palmas was thus the first colonial city in Spain.

The tour begins at the main bus station in San Telmo, at the **Estación de Guagas de San Telmo,** which can be reached in 4 ways.

1st possibility: From the jetty you walk the Muelle Santa Catalina towards the city. On the left side is the small box of the tourist information, in front of which the Hop-On Hop- Off buses start. Now turn left and come to a large square covered by a triangular awning. Among them is the city's central bus station.

Take the elevator, which is located in the left glass box to the bus station below, or take the staircase further to the right. Bus lines 30 and 91 run every 10-15 minutes to the Estación de Guagas de San Telmo. The journey takes 15 minutes, the tickets amounting to € 1.40 can be purchased directly from the bus driver. ①Further information can be found at www.guaguasglobal.com

2nd possibility: A taxi will take you to the old town of Vegueta in about 15 minutes. The ride costs about € 10.00. The taxi stand is on the right, at the El Muelle shopping centre. Depending on your destination, you can also take a bus to the bus station Estación de Guagas de San Telmo, the market hall Mercado de Veguetaor the cathedral Catedral Basílica de Santa Ana and start your tour of the old town.

3rd possibility: The Hop-on Hop- Off Bus offers a nice sightseeing tour, stops also in Vegueta for a small free English guided tour of the old town. With a current price of € 28.00 per person, this bus ride is expensive just to get to Vegueta.

4th possibility: From the jetty you come to the small box of the tourist information, from where you turn left and follow the coastal road. After approx. 5 km on foot you meet the former island capital La Vuegeta, where life pulsates in the district Triana.

The Guiniguada Gorge, through which today the street GC-5 runs, divides the founding town into 2 parts: In Vegueta there were the large townhouses, churches and government buildings, in Triana there were houses of merchants, the middle class and workers, most of whom came from Andalusia, as well as large gardens and smaller religious buildings. Triana was the part of the historic centre that changed the most over the centuries and the starting point for the first urban expansion with squares, cultural facilities and modern buildings that far surpassed colonial architecture.

At the bus station **Estación de Guagas de San Telmo [1]** you cross inland the Avenida Rafael Cabrera, above which the **Parque de San Telmo [2]** is located. For centuries, this square marked the end of the city and the beginning of the port area. In the course of the urban expansion, the port activities were stopped and the square was transformed into a small park that served as a link between the old town of Vegueta and the new district of Triana.

The central point of the square is the **Kiosko de la Música [3]**, a picturesque pavilion in and in front of which music events occasionally take place.

To the left of the square is the **Ermita de San Telmo [4]**. The chapel dates from the 17th century and is one of the oldest buildings in the city. With its altarpieces and the elaborate Mudejar wooden ceiling, it is one of the most beautiful in the archipelago.

Behind it lies the tourist information **Punto de Información Turistica** in a small pavilion, where among other things city maps are available.☉ Mon-Sun 9-14 o'clock, closed on 25.12/ 01.01 and 06.01. ① Alternatively, you can download the city maps at www.LPAvisit.com .

To the right of the square is the **Kiosko Modernista [5]**, an Art Nouveau kiosk that was dismantled in Valencia in 1924 and rebuilt on the square. The Canarios meet here to drink a café on the lively terrace in front of the kiosk and watch the hustle and bustle on the square.

Above the square is the **Gobierno Militar [6],** where the military government has its seat. From here, turn left along Calle Mayor de Triana, the district's shopping street.

"Trinear" - shopping in Triana, with specialist shops, restaurants and bars, is one of the most popular leisure activities of the inhabitants.

At the end, the road forks into Calle San Pedro and Calle Mendizábal. Now follow the left fork (Mendizábal) and at the end on the left side you meet the **Teatro Peréz Galdos [7]**. It is the most important theatre in the capital and one of the most modern in Spain since its complete renovation in 2007. The first theatre under the name Teatro Cairasco was not built until the middle of the 19th century, but it was destroyed in a major fire in 1918 and rebuilt in 1921. It was finally completed in 1928 by Miguel Martín- Fernández de la Torre, who won over his brother Nestór, the main painter of the Canary Islands, for the interior design. The pompous theatre has 1007 seats and the orchestra can be raised up to 88 musicians. ① Guided 1-hour tours through the premises are available in English and Spanish. ☼ Mon-Fri 10.15/ 11.15/ 12.15 🎫 5€, the ticket counter is located right next to the main entrance in a concrete block with the inscription Taquillas.

On the opposite side of the theatre is the **Mercado de Vegueta [8],** and you also cross the 4-lane expressway. Behind the reddish-brown façade with green doors is the Vegueta market, where fresh island produce is offered. It is the first market hall of the city, which was opened in 1787. ☼ Mon-Thu 6.30-14 o'clock, Fr-Sat 6.30-15 o'clock, closed on Sundays.

Follow Calle Mendizábal until you reach Calle Montesdeoca, then turn left into Calle Agustín Millares and finally arrive at the **Iglesia de San Agustín [9]**. The church was built by the Town Council in 1524 as a thanksgiving for an epidemic that had struck the island, and it was originally a simple hermitage, the Ermita de la Vera Cruz. It was dedicated to Cristo de la Vera Cruz- the crucified Jesus Christ, the patron saint of the city. After several renovations it became the main parish church of Las Palmas and the island. Worth seeing: The blue shrine above the altar with the Santísimo Cristo de la Vera Cruz. The statue of Virgen de los Dolores, the painful Virgin Mary, also known as "La Genovesa" because it was made in the Italian city of Genoa in 1747. The statue of Nuestra Señora del Carmen, the Virgin Mary with the Child Jesus in her arms, dates from 1815 and is the most venerated saint in Vegueta.

The church borders the **Palacio de Justicia**, the Palace of Justice, whose entrance is under the high bell tower of volcanic stone and surrounding wooden balcony. Now turn right into Calle Doctor Chil, with its well-kept historic buildings and typical Canarian wooden balconies. On your left you will see the **Iglesia de San Francisco de Borja [10],** the church of St. Francis of Borja, which is only open during the Mass. It is characterised by an elaborately worked entrance portal with laterally turned columns and an exploded gable triangle and represents the high phase of religious baroque architecture in the Canary Islands. After 30 years of construction it was inaugurated on 25.02.1754.☉ Mon-Sat 12.30 o'clock, Sun+holidays 11 o'clock

Further up the street, on the corner of Calle Dr. Verneau, on the left-hand side is the **Museo Canario [11]**, the Canarian Museum with the picture of a skull and crossbones on the corner façade. Founded in 1879 in Las Palmas, it is the most important archaeological museum in the Canary Islands, with the most complete collections on the indigenous people of Gran Canaria. Particularly interesting is the exhibition of several mummies and skulls, as well as the ceramic collection with clay vessels, which is marked with geometric motifs. ☉ Mon-Fri 10-20 Uhr, Sat-Sun+public holidays 10-14 Uhr, 25.12/ 01.01 closed ♦€5,00, children up to 12 years free For ⓘthe free audioguide an identification document must be deposited.

Back down the road, turn left into Calle Reloj and you will see the **Catedral Basílica de Santa Ana [12]** on your right. In 1483, after the conquest of Gran Canaria, the Castilian crown ordered the construction of the Cathedral in order to missionize the defeated natives. The construction work begun in the 15th century continued into the 19th century, so that the interior of the church was decorated with Roman and Gothic elements and a neoclassical façade. Santa Ana is the oldest and largest church on the island and was the only cathedral on the islands until the Canary Islands were divided into the dioceses of Gran Canaria and Tenerife in 1819.

The long **Plaza de Santa Ana[13]** is located in front of the main portal of the cathedral. This square was chosen by the conquerors as the centre around which further development was to take place. Right at the beginning there are 8 life-size cast iron **dog statues,** the work of the French sculptor Alfred Jacquemar from 1895. According to tradition, the islands owe their name to the dogs (lat. canis = dogs) which were free running at that time.

In front of you is the imposing **Casa Consistorial**, built in neoclassical style and inaugurated in 1856. Until the transfer of the mayor's office to Las Palmas in 1977, the building functioned as a town hall. It currently serves as an exhibition space for 90 paintings by Canarian and international artists and houses the tourist information office.

In the right block is the simple **Palacio Episcopal** from the 16th century with the seat of the bishop. **The Archivo Histórico Provincial** is located in the left block, house no. 4. It was the residence of the first important Canarian historian José de Viera y Claijo (1731-1813).

To the right of the entrance to the Cathedral's main portal is the paid **elevator** that leads to a panoramic terrace from which you can enjoy a magnificent view over the Old Town. Other staircases, next to the elevator on the upper floor, lead to the church tower, from where you have the most beautiful view over Las Palmas.

Access to the church outside of the fair is only possible via the **Museo Diocesano de Arte Sacro [14],** which is signposted, to the right in Calle Espíritu Santo, in a side entrance on the left. The Museum of Sacred Art is located in the former outbuildings of the Cathedral, the centre of which is the so-called Patio de los Naranjos, the inner courtyard of the orange trees with surrounding wooden balustrades. In the 4 exhibition rooms, of which the Sala Capitular is the most magnificent, goldsmith's work, monstrances, crosses and liturgical objects from the 16th century are exhibited. The Puerta del Aire, the air door leads into the cathedral. ☉ Mon-Fri 10-16.30, Sat 10-13.30, Sun+holidays closed ♨ tower € 1,50, museum/ cathedral € 3,00

Go down the street and you will find the crossing Calle Reyes Católicos, where there is a market every Sunday between 10.00 and 14.00 hrs. Now turn left and you will automatically arrive at **Casa de Colón [15]**, the Columbus house with the Plaza de Pilar Nuevo in front of it. The square is adorned by a pretty stone fountain, which was the meeting place of the women who drew water here. The magnificent façade of the Columbus House captivates with a portal made of light green lava stone with leaf ornaments and two dogs on the side consoles. Typical Canarian wooden balconies round off the appearance.

OPTIONAL, Calle de los Balcones on the right leads to **Centro Atlántico de Arte [16]**, CAAM for short. It is the cultural centre and art museum of the capital. Behind a neoclassical façade, which is currently decorated with colourful geometric elements, there are 5 floors of bright, modern exhibition rooms lined up around a typical Canarian patio. The centre primarily exhibits avant-garde art and has a collection of works by artists who had a major influence on the 20th century Canarian art scene.☉ Tue-Sat 10-21, Sun+ holidays 10- 14 h, Mon/ 24.12/ 31.12 closed ♦Admission free ①Current exhibitions at: www.caam.net

The entrance to the Columbus House is on the opposite side of the street, to which you come on the right through the Passage Pedro de Algaba to the **Plaza de San Antonio Abad** with the **Ermita de San Antonio Abad** of the same name (house no. 10) **[17]**. The city was founded on this square on 24 June 1478, after the Spanish general Juan Rejón arrived with his troops in the bay of Isleta. The military church built by the conquerors was converted into a hermitage. Although it was small, it served as the first parish church and later as the cathedral of Las Palmas. With the construction of the new cathedral Santa Ana it lost its importance and became known as Ermita de San Antonio Abad. Although the clergy gave the hermitage a new entrance gate in 1743, the building became increasingly dilapidated and was gutted and rebuilt in 1757. The stone tablet on the façade recalls Cristóbal Colón - Christopher Columbus, who prayed here before his departure into the New World.

From here, turn left into **Calle Colón** to **Casa de Colón**. The Columbus House was the house of the island governor and functions as a museum whose central theme is Christopher Columbus and his travels. On his way to America in 1492, Columbus visited the house when he anchored off the island to have one of his ships repaired. In the 1950s the building was converted into the Museo Casa de Cólon, integrating parts of the old Governor's Palace and the imposing portal into the complex. The museum has 15 exhibition rooms and 2 inner courtyards, of which the larger one has a Gothic fountain. The arches are Renaissance and the wooden balustrade comes from the Dominican monastery destroyed by pirates in the 16th century. The ground floor provides a historical overview of the discoverer's travels. Worth seeing are the models of his caravels Niña, Pinta and the flagship of his expedition, the Santa Maria. The overall picture is completed by nautical charts and routes as well as the replica of the captain's cabin. Information and exhibits from the time when the islands were a stopover on the way to the "new world" will also be presented. On the upper floor there are paintings from the 16th - 20th centuries, as well as objects, models and maps of the history of Gran Canaria and the capital Las Palmas. In the basement a collection of art and utensils of pre-Columbian peoples of Latin America has been collected. ☉ Mon-Sat 10-18, Sun+holidays 10-15 ♪ €4,00

You go back to the museum entrance. Now you reach on the left the adjoining Calle Armas to the 4-lane street, which you cross again and come to a large place, the Plaza de las Ranas with massive rubber trees. The building to the right of the Burger King fast food chain houses the **Biblioteca Insular [18]**. It is one of the best examples of Canarian architecture at the end of the 19th century. At that time, the building was used in different ways and was reformed several times until it was converted into an island library.

If you keep left parallel to the main road, you will come to Calle Muro, which becomes Calle General Bravo. On the right is the Plaza Cairasco with the monument to the grancanarian writer and poet Cairasco de Figueroa (1538-1610). At that time he was the founder of Canarian literature. In his works he combines the historical past of the Canary Islands, which was shaped by the natives and later by the conquerors.

It stands in front of the **Gabinete Literario [19],** the cabinet of literature that housed the first theatre in the city and was initially named after Cairasco, who had his residence here. A literary society founded in 1844 bought the building, which still contributes to literary, cultural and scientific development today. The elaborately designed façade with central balconies and side towers makes the cabinet appear elegant. The rounded side facades are conspicuous, giving the building size and infinity. Above the balcony there is the lion's coat of arms of the partnership with the initials GL and above the windows there is a border on which tiles with a palm tree and a dog are depicted at regular intervals. These motives lead back to the island conquerors, who came across palm trees and free running dogs. In the foyer, the imposing central entrance staircase leads up to the upper floor with a gallery all around, to which the Salon Rojo, a coffee and tea room and the theatre hall are connected. In the Salon Rojo, the red salon, the coats of arms of the 50 Spanish provinces were applied, besides, portraits of the founders, as well as that of the artist Peréz Galdos most important after Cevantes decorate the walls. The adjoining room captivates with columns and a light yellow wall colour. The large windows with lead glass inlays lend the area an elegant chic. In the middle of the room there is access to the balcony overlooking the Cathedral of Santa Ana. The real highlight is the former theatre, which was based on a small Versailles. The walls abound with elaborately embedded column constructions, gold ornaments, wall and ceiling paintings. The orchestra played from a balcony on the upper floor. The glory and glory of the upper class have been preserved in this magnificent room. Another highlight of the building is the still intact elevator, which was the first elevator of the island and reminds of the pure luxury of those times. Currently, the private library of the literature cabinet is located on the 2nd floor, which can only be used by members. ◑ Guided tours at 10.15/ 11.15/ 12.15 ♪€ 5,00 ⓦwww.cityexpert.travel

On the right, in the row of houses next to the Gabinete Literario, is the **Hotel Madrid** from 1908, where the Spanish General Franco is said to have stayed overnight on his way to Morocco in 1936.

On the opposite square, the **Plaza de San Francisco [20]**, the **Alameda de Colón** stands in the middle, a monument from the year 1892, which commemorates the stay of Christopher Columbus before his Atlantic crossing.

Behind it is the **Iglesia de San Francisco de Asís [21]**. The parish was founded in 1821 and is located in the church of the former monastery of San Francisco. The three naves and the Mudejár coffered ceilings were built in the typical style of the country. In this church, the Shrine of the Virgin Mary of Nuestra Señora de la Soledad, our Lady of Solitude, is venerated by the inhabitants of Las Palmas. Apart from the statues of San Francisco de Asís, San Bernadino de Siena and Santa Clara de Asís, the Nuestra Señora de la Soledad is the only image of the Virgin Mary to receive the canonical coronation of Blessed John Paul XXIII in the diocese of the Canary Islands.

If you now turn right into Calle Malteses, which was named in the 16th century after the local merchants from Malta, and then turn left into Calle Cano, you will find the **Casa Museo Peréz Galdos [22]** in the 3rd building on the right (house no.6). The building dates from the 18th century and was the birthplace of the Canarian novelist Benito Peréz Galdós (1843-1920), who spent his childhood and youth. The municipal theatre in Plaza Stagno was named after him. The museum exhibits novels from that period, original documents and documents written by the artist himself. ◑ Tue-Sun 10-18 h, Mon, 25.12/ 31.12/ 01.01/ 06.01/ 01.05. Closed ♪ Admission free

Follow the road and you will see the **Librería del Calbildo [23]** on the corner of Calle Travieso. It is the first bookstore in the archipelago to specialise in Canarian themes and authors, providing more than 5,000 titles.

Follow Calle Cano to the end and turn left into Calle San Bernado. At the corner you can see the impressive grey-white building (house no. 8) of the **Círculo Mercantil [24]** from the 17th century. Free leisure and cultural events, which are appreciated by the inhabitants of the town, are held in the complex by the Canary Islands Trade District.
Then take the next street Calle Pérez Galdos to the right and you will see the **Palacete Rodríguez Queguez [25]** on your right. At the end of the 19th century, the elderly merchant Domingo Rogríguez Quereles decided to build a large house and commissioned the famous Gran Canaria architect Fernando Navarro y Navarro with the planning. He designed a magnificent building that reflected the modern zeitgeist of this epoch. Currently it is the seat of the higher music conservatory.

Straight ahead, at the junction with Calle de Perdomo, stands the **Iglesia de los Franciscanos [26]** with a striking Baroque stone façade.
If you follow the road down and turn left into Calle Viera y Clavijo, you will find the **Teatro Cuyas [27]** in the building number 30. The theatre is one of the most important stages in the Canary Islands. It is one of the best national theatres in Spain with first-class stage equipment, a capacity of 943 seats and a varied programme of events.
At the next intersection, turn into Calle Domingo J. Navarro and you will find **FEDAC [28]**, the Fundación para la Etnografia y el Desarollo de la Artesania Canaria on the right-hand side of building number 7. The souvenir shop run by the municipality offers certified handicrafts.© Mon-Fri 10.30-13.30/ 16.30-20 h, Sat+ Sun closed

At the end of the street you will come to the main shopping street, Calle Mayor de Triana, which you follow to the left until you reach the starting point of the itinerary.

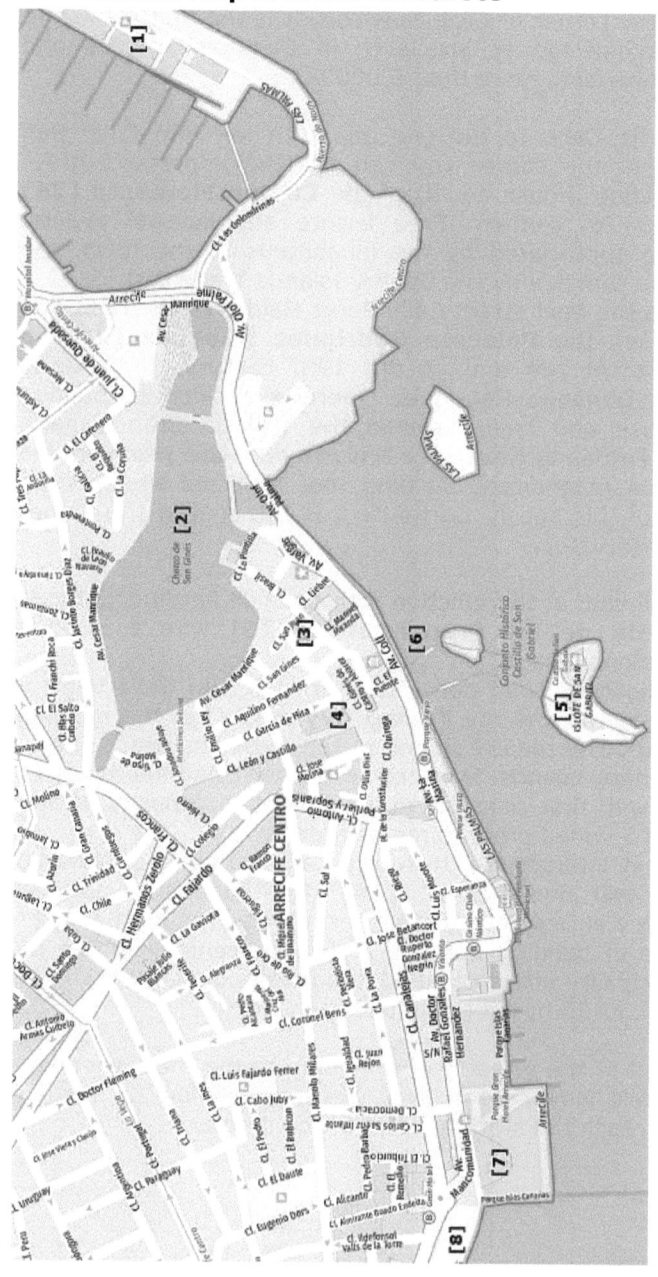

15 Welcome to the capital Arrecife on Lanzarote!

You have now anchored in the harbour on the 4th largest island with 846 sqkm. Lanzarote has a total population of 146,000, of whom 57,000 live in the capital. At your arrival it must be mentioned that there are two moorings depending on the traffic.

Your cruise ship moors either in the old port, the Puerto de Los Marmóles, or in the new port at the Marina Lanzarote.

From the **Puerto de Los Marmóles** there is a free bus transfer from the boat to the parking lot in front of the Charco de San Ginés. From the container of the Tourist Information, with the inscription Turismo Arrecife, which is on the right hand side, follow Calle Juan de Quesada to the left, which leads to **Charco de San Ginés [2]**.

At the exit of the new port, Avenida Olof Palme leads to the Charco de San Ginés. Along the high quay walls you follow the road and meet the long concrete building of the **Marina Lanzarote [1]** on the right side. If you now turn right at car park P3 with the tourist information and turn left, you will reach the shopping mile of the marina, which leads past the newly designed marina. The modern complex was designed more than generously for Lanzarote conditions, but was not accepted, so that many shops and cafés had to close.

At the end of the promenade you come to a larger square and cross the bridge over the harbour basin.

You will come to Avenida Olof Palme, which you follow to the right and then cross the crosswalk that leads you across the road to **Charco de San Ginés [2]**. Follow the promenade on the right and you will come to the bridge over the Charco.

If you follow the promenade before the bridge, you can walk around the entire Charco. Here you have the possibility to walk right along the promenade, the Avenida César Manrique, and choose one of the countless local restaurants to taste the typical tapas of the island, or simply take a seat to enjoy the view of the Charco, which means "puddle of holy ginés", with a drink. Alternatively, cross the bridge immediately and turn right.

Follow the signs along the Charco. After the slight left bend, turn right into Calle La Puntilla, which at the end makes a left-right bend and turn left into Calle Brasil, which you follow. Now you already see the high 3-storey bell tower of the church San Ginés.

The **Iglesia de San Ginés [3]** was founded in 1574 as the first pilgrimage chapel in the capital and had to be rebuilt after the great flooding in 1665 with a construction period of two years. After another 80 years, in 1747, it was enlarged, until finally in 1798, when it received its present status as a parish. In the 19th century it was enlarged by a main nave, a central nave was added, so that ten years later, when the pulpit was raised, a high nave was built. After further 40 years the church tower was built, which was finished 1842. ☉daily 9-13 and 17-20 o'clock.

At the picturesque church square Plaza de las Palmas, which is planted with Indian laurel trees and palm trees, you follow the Calle Inspector Luis Martín, which leads to the main shopping street Calle Léon y Castillo, at the Café El Principe in front of it. The yellow tiled building **Casa Amarilla [4]** is located directly above the corner. The building was the former seat of the island government, which was built in the 1920s, declared a cultural asset of special interest in 2002 and renovated in 2014. In the exhibition rooms temporally changing presentations take place, which reflect the history of the island. ☉ Mon-Fri 10- 22 o'clock, Sat 10- 14 o'clock ♨ € 2,00 ①Current exhibition under: www.cactlanzarote.com

The 500 m long **Calle Léon y Castillo** with its many side streets is the most visited shopping mile of the capital, where you can shop and drink a café among the locals. The city walk leads left at the Casa Amarilla, towards the sea on the Avenida la Marina.

In front of you you will come to the bridge Calle Puente de la Lagarta, which leads to the castle **Castillo San Gabriel [5]** with the museum **Museo de Historia de Arrecife.** The castle can also be reached via a second bridge on the left.

This is called **Puente de las Bolas [6]** and is a small drawbridge with two cannonballs on the pillars. It was originally built of wood and burnt down by Berber pirates. In the 16th century the Castillo was replaced by a stone fortress to protect the port and the town. The museum guide is handed out at the entrance, where the English explanations to the overview boards can be found in the various rooms of the castle. Enjoy the unique view over the sea and the capital on the upper floor. ☉ Mon-Fri 10-17 h, Sat 10-14 h ♨ Free admission

Go back to the promenade of Avenida Marina and follow the road to the left.

Along the sea, past the small park Parque José Ramírez Cerda, the rustic wooden pavilion of the tourist information office - Oficina de Información Turística - the Avenida la Marina changes into Calle Blas Cabrera Felipe and after a right turn becomes Calle Dr. Ruperto González Negrín. Follow the road and you will automatically reach the **Gran Hotel Arrecife [7]**. It is the highest and most striking building on the island. On the 17th floor there is a public café with a unique view. You have a view over the capital, volcanic mountains, the coastline and, with good visibility, the neighbouring island of Fuerteventura.➀ **Important:** For the <u>public café of</u> the 5-star hotel there is no separate entrance from outside. You enter the hotel via the main entrance and head for the reception, which you pass on your right. In the corridor you pass the toilets on the left and then go up the stairs on the left. The glass elevator to the café is immediately on the left.

The 500 m long bright city beach **Playa de Reducto [8]** borders directly on the Gran Hotel and invites to swim at high tide. Sunbeds and umbrellas are not free, but the beach offers enough space to enjoy the sun with your own towel.

This is where the city tour ends. Alternatively, you can take a taxi from the Gran Hotel to the jetty in the Marina Lanzarote,or to the meeting point at the Charco de San Ginés,or then back to the boat. ➘ Taxi Gran Hotel- Ship to Marina max. €10, Gran Hotel- Puerto de los Marmóles, max. € 15.

<u>Alternatively you can</u> explore the capital Arrecife with the **Hop On Hop Off** train. Entry points are located directly at the tourist information at the Charco de Ginés and at the end of the Marina Lanzarote. City Sightseeing Arrecife offers 2 tours which can be used in one day with the ticket. **Red line:** Charco San Ginés- Intercambiador de Guaguas, bus station - Gran Hotel Arrecife- Real Club Nautico- Castillo San Gabriel- Marina Lanzarote, marina - Castillo San José. **Blue line:** Charco San Ginés- Castillo San José- Estacion de Guagas, bus station- Teatro insular, city theatre- Gran Hotel Arrecife- Real Club Nautico- Castillo San Gabriel- Marina Lanzarote. Entry and exit can take place as often as you like, the fare is due once at the start of the journey. You will receive a city map and headphones that provide interesting and informative information about the tour's sights during the tour.➒ Daily➲ € 10,00, children 7-12 y. € 6,00, 3-7 y. € 4,00 Entrance to Castillo San José is included in ➀the fare.

The **Castillo San José** served as a military fortress and houses the International Museum of **Contemporary** Art, the **Museo Internacional de Arte Contemporáneo MIAC**, and was built in the 18th century during the reign of the Bourbon Carlos III.

On the initiative of the outstanding island artist César Manrique, who had a lasting influence on the island, the dilapidated building was redesigned according to his plans and opened in 1975. The artist personally led the reconstruction work and the development, but hardly changed the internal structure of the castle. In the outbuildings, Manrique designed a restaurant that represents the most striking intervention in the architecture of the old fortress. Access to the building is via the old drawbridge. Impressive are the meter-thick vaulted walls in which temporary art exhibitions are located. Follow the stairs to the upper floor, look out from the industrial port - Muelle de Los Mármoles -, up to the 5 star Gran Hotel Arrecife.

The QUÉ MUAC restaurant is located in the basement, which can be reached by a curved staircase, where you can dine, drink a café or simply enjoy the view of the harbour.

On this way a short detour to the **Jolateros would** also be interesting. Before the Castillo San José, follow the main road to the left and you will see a large windmill on your right. Until the 20th century this was used to extract salt water from the sea, to transport it and to extract salt here in the form of salt pans.

A few steps further you will find the open-air workshop.

At first sight I had not understood what was being done here until Mr. Antonio explained his work to me. The history of the Jolateros, the only and last Lanzarote boatbuilders to produce 1-man boats from scrap metal, goes back about 70-80 years. In the past, these small boats were built for the purpose of taking the fishermen to their cutters. Nowadays the children only organize small boat races in the Charco San Ginés in summer.

Then Señor Antonio showed how to make the boats in miniature. For this purpose he cut a strip from a tin can of olive oil with scissors. He took a pair of pliers, bent the sharp edges inwards and then knocked them flat on a wooden board. Then he formed the shape of the boat with his thumbs and fingers, took an adhesive and spread it on two small pieces of wood and put them on the ends of the boat to fix them.

He said: "Now I'm doing the final test to see if the boat can swim". He put it in a plastic bowl with water and I was amazed... the boat floated. Finally, the small work of art is given an individual coat of paint and is ready for sale.

This old Lanzarote boat building art is worth seeing. Here you can buy a **souvenir** of a special kind. The small boats can also be purchased as key rings for a small price.

Space for your own notes✏... ...

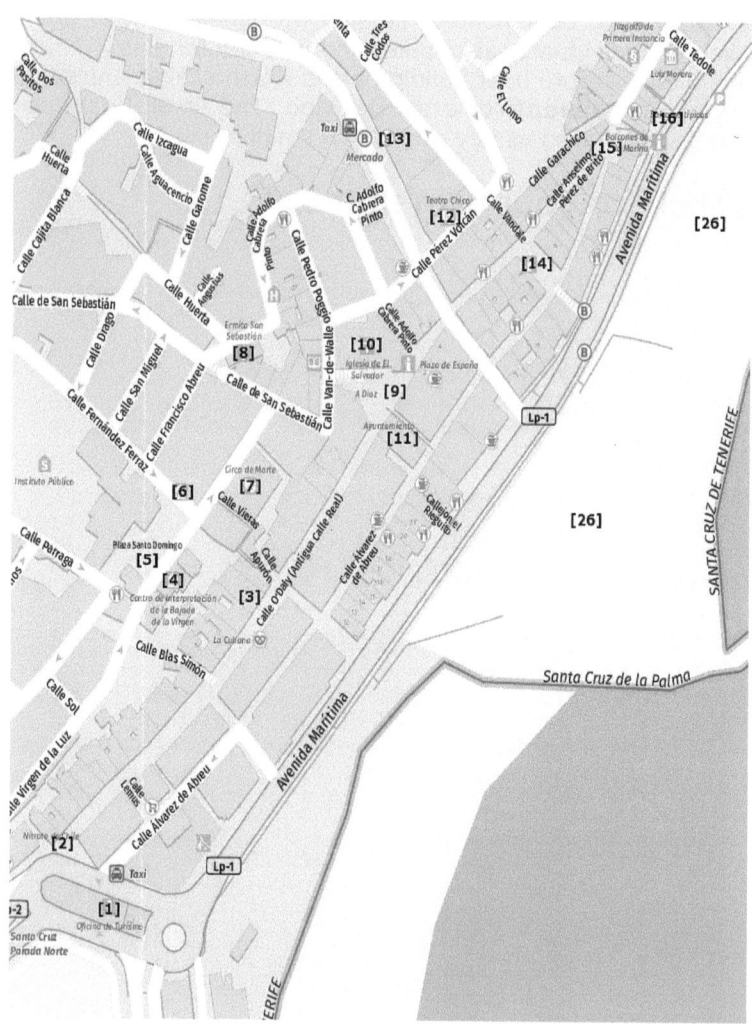

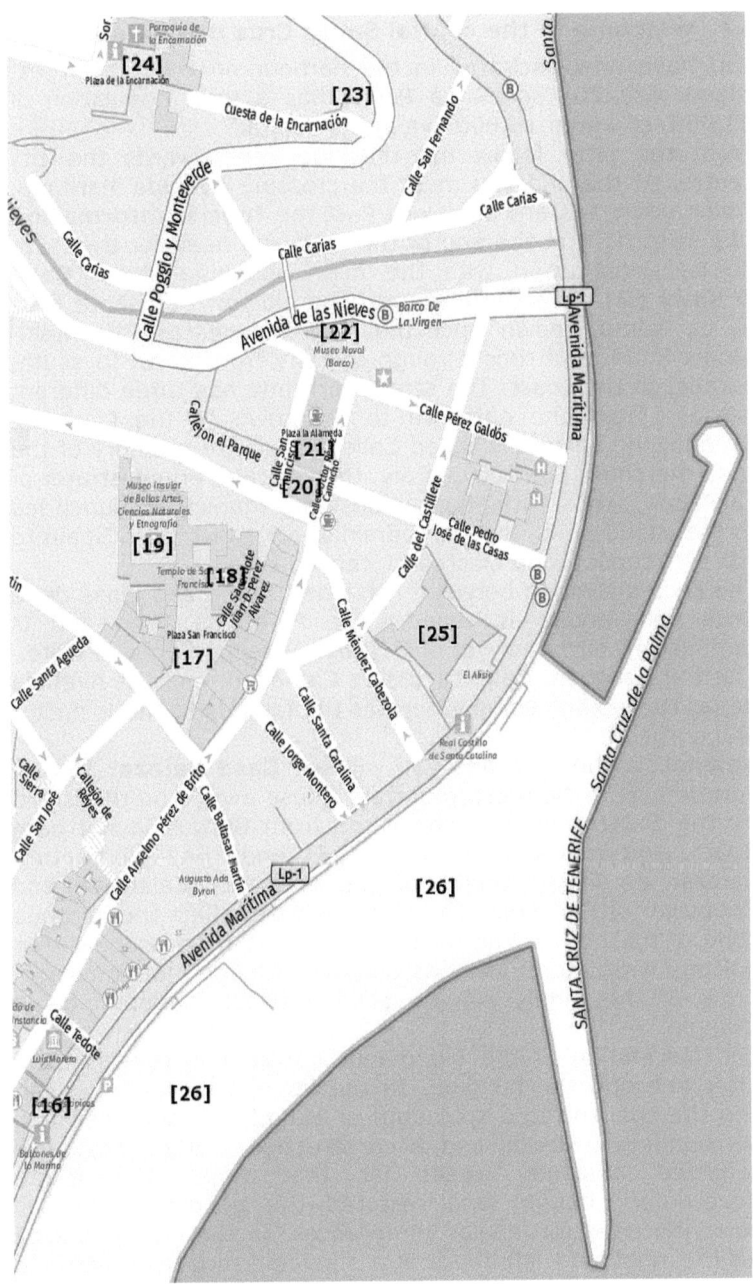

Parroquía de
la Encarnación

[24]

Plaza de la Encarnación

Calle Sor

Cuesta de la Encarnación

[23]

Calle San Fernando

Calle Carías

Calle Poggío y Monteverde

Calle Carías

Calle Nieves

Calle Carías

Calle Carías

Avenida de las Nieves

[22]

Barco De
La Virgen

Museo Naval
(Barco)

Lp-1

Avenida Marítima

Callejón en el Parque

Calle Pérez Galdós

Plaza la Alameda

[21]

[20]

Calle del Castillete

Calle Pedro
José de las Casas

Museo Insular
de Bellas Artes,
Ciencías Naturales
y Etnografía

[19]

Calle San Francisco

Calle Anselmo Camacho

Templo de San
Francisco

[18]

Calle San Telmo de
Juan D. Pérez
Álvarez

Plaza San Francisco

[17]

Calle Méndez Cabezola

[25]

El Altar

Real Castillo
de Santa Catalina

Calle Santa Águeda

Calle San José

Calle
Sierra

Callejón de
Reyes

Calle Anselmo Pérez de Brito

Calle Baltasar Martín

Calle Jorge Montero

Calle Santa Catalina

Augusto Ada
Byron

Lp-1

Avenida Marítima

[26]

Santa Cruz de la Palma

SANTA CRUZ DE TENERIFE

de
Instancia

Calle Tedote

Luis Moreno

[16]

Balcones de
la Marina

[26]

45

17 Welcome to the capital Santa Cruz de La Palma!

You have now anchored in the harbour on the 5th largest island with 708 sqkm. La Palma has a total population of 83,000, of whom 16,000 live in the capital.

From the jetty follow the red-blue line towards the city centre. At the end you meet the crossing Avenida Marítima, which you cross and turn left. Past the **tourist information [1]**, turn right at the end of the road and head for the Plaza de La Constitución with the main shopping street **Calle O´Daly [2]**. It is the lifeline of the old town of Santa Cruz de La Palma, known since the earliest times as Calle Real-King's Road, and runs through the city from north to south, parallel to the coast. The street currently has three different names: From the entrance to the town to the Plaza de España, the section is called Calle O´Daly. In memory of the Irish merchant Dionisio O´Daly, the fiduciary administrator of La Palma, whose litigation against the municipal council led to the island being the first administrative district in Spain to have its constitution elected by census vote.

The second section between Plaza de España and Plaza de la Cruz del Tercero is called Calle Pérez de Brito and is reminiscent of the lawyer of O´Daly, Anselmo Pérez de Brito.

The third section, Calle Dr. Pérez Camacho, ends at Avenida de las Nieves and commemorates the famous Palmeric doctor and surgeon.

Now follow the road and you will see **Casa Salazar [3]** on your left. It is the most important house owned on the island by the Salazar family, who came from Burgos in northern Spain, and was built between 1631 and 1642 by Ventura Salazar de Frias, Knight of the Order of Calatrava and Councillor of La Palma. The stone ashlars reflect the baroque style of the house. The façade is adorned by a wrought-iron balcony with lateral columns above which the marble coat of arms of the family can be seen between an open gable triangle.

The fascination of the old manor house only reveals itself after entering the building. In the inner courtyard you can see the concentrated splendour of Mujader wooden ceilings, surrounding galleries and a construction method that also reflected absolute wealth at that time. The island government bought and restored the building, which is currently used for insular conferences. In the entrance area on the right and left there is a souvenir shop with certified handmade art. ☻ Mon-Fri 9-14 and 16-21 h, Sat 9-14 h,

Sundays closed 🕭Entrance free ⌂ Calle O´Daly, 22 ⓘThe inner courtyard and the 1st floor are accessible, the upper part of the building is not accessible.

Optional: If you take the next road to the left into Calle Apurón, you will come to the parallel road Virgen de La Luz with the following sights: The **Centro de Interpretación Bajada de la Virgen [4]** is located in house no. 13 in the row of houses on the left. The new Interpretation Centre shows and explains the most important festival in the capital. Every 5 years, from June to August, Santa Cruz celebrates the Bajada de la Virgen de las Nieves in honour of the island's patron saint. In 1676, the inhabitants of the island carried the statue of the Virgin Mary of Las Nieves down to the city to implore the intercession of the Blessed Virgin to bring to an end the terrible period of drought under which the landscape, people and livestock had suffered for far too long. Thus the bishop García Ximénez issued the ecclesiastical decree that this pious act should be repeated every five years from 1680 onwards.

On the second Sunday in July the Semana Grande, the big week of the Bajada, starts with the procession of the Mascarones, the giants and stubheads, who represent fairy tale figures like the Bruja, the witch, and also current comic figures. Since 1945, Wednesday has been dedicated to the minuet, whose music was written by the Palmeric composer Luis Cobiella Cuevas. The dance event alludes to the splendour and elegance of rococo in the 18th century. The undeniable highlight of the festival takes place on Thursday of the same week with La Danza de los Enanos, the dwarf dance whose origins can be traced back to the Corpus Christi celebrations of 1833. At the end of the exhibition, you can take an interactive photo of yourself, which will automatically appear on the Museum Facebook page. ◑ Mon-Fri 10-15 h, Sat 10-13 h, Sun closed 🕭 € 4,50 Combined ticket with the Museo Naval € 7,00 ⌂ Calle Virgen de La Luz, 13

Raised on the left is the square with the church **Plaza e Iglesia de Santo Domingo [5]**. At the confluence of Calle Virgen de la Luz and Calle Fernándes Ferraz steps lead to the Plaza, which is dominated by 2 large Indian laurel trees. To the left, next to the two semi-circular doors with a covered wooden balcony, is the Instituto de Enseñanza Secundaria, the College of Teacher Education. The church of Santo Domingo, located in the same façade on the right, is closed. During fairs, Flemish works of art from the 16th and 17th centuries, brought to the island by Dutch merchants, can be admired inside the church.

On the right is the **Educación- Germán González Museum [6]**. The Museum of Educational History is a tribute to Germán González, the main advocate of public education in Santa Cruz, who died in 2011. While still alive, he was awarded the prestigious Viera y Clavijo Prize in 2000. The premises present an old Canarian classroom with furniture, textbooks and educational material used in the 20th century.

🕐 Mon-Fri 10-14 h 🎫 Admission free

Follow Calle Virgen de La Luz to the right and you will see the light blue and white building of the **Teatro Circo de Marte [7]** on your right. At that time the building served as a venue for cockfights and circus performances. It opened in 1871 and was restored between 1914 and 1918. Today concerts and theatre events take place in the rooms. Directly opposite is the Taquilla for ticket sales. If you follow the road, turn left at the end and go up Calle San Sebastián, which leads to the square of the same name with the chapel **Plaza San Sebastián y Ermita [8]**. It was the main road that ran through the district and carried the leg name La Canela, which is due to the production of cinnamon desserts. It was named after the holy Roman martyr Sebastian, the patron saint against the plague. The road was part of the Camino Real, the Royal Road that connected the capital with the valley of Aridane and the port of Tazacorte. The Ermita was built in the 16th century and has typical island architecture: The main entrance, wooden balcony and bell tower lie on one axis above the other. It can be visited during the fair. On the bench in front of the church you can enjoy the magic of the quarter with a wonderful sea view.

Back to main shopping street O´Daly.

If you now follow the road upwards, Calle O´Daly changes to Calle Real, which is wider and on the left side you will find **Plaza de España [9]** with **Iglesia de Salvador [10]**. The main square of Santa Cruz has always had a double function throughout its history. It was the public square of the Iglesia de El Salvador, the Church of the Redeemer, and at the same time the venue for the city's most important celebrations. The festival in honour of the patron saints, the founding ceremony of the capital, Corpus Christi, Holy Week and Christmas take place here. At the beginning of the 19th century it was called Plaza de La Constitución, the constitutional square, to commemorate the first Spanish constitution signed in Cádiz in 1814. Furthermore, it is also known as Plaza del Consistorio, Municipal and Town Hall Square and Plaza de la Iglesia, Church Square. Its present name is Plaza de España. The trapezoidal square, the church, the opposite town hall and the town houses form a unique unity in the Canary Islands in Renaissance style.

The Monteverde building, number 1, was built by Pablo Monteverde in 1618 and was restored between 1922 and 1935. House number 2 is the Lorenzo building, built in the 18th century classicist style and reformed in 1900. The Saviour's Church with its volcanic stone bell tower dates back to the 15th century and was completed in the 16th century. In the building Massieu, with the house number 4 from the 18th century is the CajaCanarias. House number 5, Casa Pereyra dates back to 1864 and was rebuilt by Miguel Pereyra Pérez.

At the centre of the square is the monument to the priest Manuel Díaz, who was an important figure in the political and cultural life of La Palma in the first half of the 19th century. The town fountain from 1588, also called La Pila, completes the square.

On the opposite side is the town hall **Ayuntamiento de Santa Cruz de La Palma [11]**. After a serious fire in 1553, the island government decided to build the new Santa Cruz Town Hall. The construction work began in 1559 and already after 8 years the new town house could be inaugurated. On the ground floor 4 archways dominate the façade, on the upper floor there are two oval and two rectangular windows. Numerous relieves and inscriptions represent the virtues and vices of the time.

Follow the road to the intersecting **Avenida del Puente**, which you cross and go up to the left. After the first crossroad, Calle Pérez Volcán, you will see on your right the **Teatro Chico [12]** with the adjacent market hall **La Recova [13]**. The small **theatre** was founded in 1866 by the company "Terpsícore y Melponeme" as a place for shows and public celebrations. The building was actually the oratory of the old Hospital Dolores y Concepción, which was founded in 1514. After the hospital was moved to the Claras nunnery in 1837, the subsequent renovation work had the aim of no longer recognising the sacred character of the building so that it could be used as a theatre. It currently serves as a cinema.

In and in front of the **La Recova** market hall, everyday life takes place between fruit and vegetables, cheese and meat counters. Benefit from the colourful variety of local products. The market hall is located on the site of the former Nuestra Señora de los Dolores Hospital, founded in 1514. The building was built in 1886 in classicist style and captivates by its horizontal linearity. The entrance gate was set into the misting masonry and decorated with a semi-circular gable. All other entrance doors are separated from each other by pilasters and lead into separate rooms, which are connected to the actual market hall, but have a separate entrance. At the right corner of the balustrade above the doors, you can see the small sculpture of San Cristóbal, Saint Christopher, patron saint of motorists and symbol of the first taxi rank in the city. The hall is illuminated by natural daylight through a window strip running under the roof. ◑ Mon-Sat 6-14 o'clock, Sun closed ⌂ Avenida del Puente, 16

Go back to the main shopping street, now called Calle Anselmo Pérez, and follow the street to the left. The Royal Yacht Club, **the Real Club Nautico, is**located on the left side of the street, house number 9. In 1817 José María Fierro Santa Cruz y Brito founded the Royal Yacht Club in his family residence. In 1904 the building was rented for the founded sports and hunting club and acquired in 1920 by the later club president. The historic building was visited in 1906 by the then Spanish King Alfonso III, who was the first King to enter the Canary Islands. Today exhibitions, literary music evenings, theatre performances, book presentations and meetings of literary circles take place here.

Continue and you will come to **Plaza de Vandale [14]** on the right. The square owes its name to the Flemish Van Dalle family, who settled on La Palma in the 16th century. The Antwerp-born Pauwel Van Dalle and Terlinxs, Lord of Lilloot, Berendrech, Zuitland and Ballert of Flanders, Knight of the Golden Spur and patron of the Saint Bernard College of the University of Leuven, was the first settler of the family.

One of the most representative buildings of the square is the house number 16, Casa Carmona, built in 1831. The lookout tower offers a beautiful view of the sea.

The square is surrounded by flame trees, which bloom red depending on the season. In the back there is a bronze sculpture called Lo Diviono. It is a tribute to Christmas music groups that sing and play every night from 13 to 24 December in the streets of the capital. This custom can be traced back to bygone times when traditional music clubs played the streets with castanets, tambourines, drums, timpani and flutes to earn Christmas bonuses for the holidays.

Opposite the square is the white house No. 15 with waving flags, where the **researchers' union** is located. It was founded in 1885 in Santa Cruz and has its seat in the former house of the Nicolás Massieu Salgado family. The building has three facades and divides the living space on three floors including the middle floor. The dust and rain catchers above the upper row of windows, crowned by marble busts and the family coat of arms, are striking. The association bought the house in 1931 and rebuilt it according to their needs.① Admission for members only

Shortly after you will see **Placeta de Borrero [15]** on your right. The small square with a basalt fountain was first mentioned by name in the 16th century and is surrounded by typical Canarian houses.

This is where the 3rd section of the shopping street begins, which is now called Calle Peréz de Brito.

From here the small street on the right, along the restaurant La Placeta, leads to the signposted **Balcones Típicos [16]**. The wooden balconies of the houses on Avenida Marítima, which are among the best preserved of their kind in the Canary Islands, are one of the capital's landmarks. In the style of Portuguese models, the balconies have always had practical uses in addition to the decorative decoration of the facades and served to supply fresh air. The backs of the houses face east towards the Atlantic, so that the inhabitants used the sea breeze to ventilate the rooms. The toilet was often installed on the balconies, so that the smell and the sewage outside the houses would run onto the street and from there into the sea.

In addition, the balconies were also used for additional control of maritime traffic in the port of Santa Cruz. In addition to the viewpoints on the roofs of the houses, the balconies offered a good view of the bay, so that the arrival and departure of the ships, the loading and unloading of the goods could be observed comfortably.

Casa Sicilia number 38: Built in the last decade of the 18th century by the priest Jerónimo Sicilia of the parish of El Salvador, the house has a closed double glazed balcony at the rear, extending over the third and fourth floors.

Casa Escobar number 39- 40: The house was built in its present state by the couple Felipe Bautista Poggio Monteverde and Maria de Escobar y Guzmán.

Casa Felipe number 41: The building was built at the beginning of the 19th century by the lieutenant of the militia and postmaster Antonio José Felipe and has remained unchanged to this day. It has an open double balcony with toilet facing north.

Casa Morales number 42: The façade of the house, built in the 2nd half of the 18th century by the silk craftsman José Antonio Morales, stands out for its asymmetrical design. The balcony is one-storey and has a prefabricated canopy and is located in the middle of the third floor.

Casa Sansón number 43: The building was built at the end of the 18th century by the silk craftsman Antonio Romualdo Sansón. The floor on which the balcony faces the sea was redesigned in the following century, after the house passed into the possession of naval captain Buenaventura Felipe Carmona, who had this balcony open and on one level.

Casa Ferrer Carta number 44: The brothers Ferrer Carta built this house at the end of the 18th century. On the front has a glazed double balcony that extends over the third and fourth floors.

Casa Ferrer number 45: The residence of the Mallorcan merchant Raimundo Ferrer was built between 1770 and 1780 and has a double balcony that runs along the entire façade. It is equipped with glass panes on the lower level and open on the upper level.

Casa Ferrer Martínez number 46: Father Antonio Ferrer Martínez built this double balcony house in the late 18th century. The lower level of the balcony is open and extends over the entire façade, while the upper level is central, closed and glazed.

You go back to the main shopping street, which you continue to follow to the right until you come to the crossing Calle Baltasar Martín. Turn left here and take the first street on your right, Calle San José. On the left you can see the **Plaza de San Francisco [17]** with the church of the same name **Paroquia de San Francisco [18]** and the island museum **Museo Insular [19]**. In 1508, the Franciscan Order founded the Real Convento de la Inmaculada Concepción, the Convent of the Immaculate Conception, and laid out the Plaza de San Francisco, the square in front of it, as a flat area. In the following 500 years, until the expropriation of the church in the 19th century, the most important religious celebrations took place here within the monastery grounds. A stone fountain, which was originally located in the lower cloister of the monastery, was planted with a tree and characterizes the appearance of the plaza. The imposing monastery was transformed into a museum.

Above the portal, the main façade of the monastery shows the replica of a vertical sundial made by the Irish merchant Teobaldo MacGhee around 1721 at his own expense.

Between the church and the monastery, the bell tower towers over a massive lava stone cladding completed in 1799. On the ground floor to the left there is the entrance gate of the monastery, which connects the antechamber with the chapel of the Venerable Third Order.

The Franciscan monks who accompanied Alonso Fernández de Lugo during the conquest of the island, after living for 15 years in straw huts, began in 1508, at the express request of Queen Juana, the construction of a monastery, the fourth of their order in the Canary Islands. The coat of arms of Castile, which can be seen in the main portal, indicates the royal patronage. Built in 1540, the Capilla de Monterrat, with its stone arch and carved coffered ceiling, is one of the earliest expressions of Renaissance art in the Canary Islands.

From the entrance under the bell tower a corridor leads to the room where the entrance tickets have to be bought. At that time it served as a porter's lodge and was seen as the filter between the urban world and the monastery. With a small bell the monks could be called to ask for recommendations and the poor came to them to ask for food. Detailed information boards in German lead through the entire complex, which presents not only a natural history and naval exhibition, but also works of art. In the adjacent José Pérez Vidal library there are antique volumes and records on display. Also worth seeing is the old courtyard, which was planted with orange trees by the Spanish Queen Sofia and the former German President Richard von Weizsäcker. ☉ Mon-Fri 9.30-19 h, Sat 10-13 h, ♦ adults: €4,00, children under 18 years free. Seniors aged 65 and over (with ID) free. Closed on public holidays, last admission 1 hour before closing.

Follow Calle San Francisco until you reach **Plazuela De La Cruz Del Tecero [20]** on your right. Between two palm trees stands the cross erected by Alonso Fernández de Lugo after his conquest in 1493. It symbolizes the foundation of the city on 03 May of that year. For the annual foundation celebrations in May, the cross is decorated with fabrics, jewellery and flowers. Next to it is the **Plaza de La Alameda [21]**. The course is surrounded by 8 large Indian laurel trees and is a popular meeting place for locals. The centre is an octagonal kiosk from the 19th century, which invites you to linger with its tables and chairs.

Behind the kiosk, towards the Columbus ship, you will discover a dwarf sculpture with Napoleon's hat, which stands as an island symbol and key figure of the peculiarities and preferences of the population. More details on this cult can be found in the Virgen de La Bajada Interpretation Centre [2]. Now you are automatically directed to the **Museo Naval- Barco De La Virgen [22]**. The ship is an exact replica of the Santa Maria, the caravel with which Christopher Columbus left La Palma in 1492 to discover the New World. Inside, it houses the Naval Museum with a collection of nautical charts, models, documents and construction plans. On the second floor there is the cabin of the famous sailor, on the bridge of the upper deck you experience the feeling to have participated actively in the discovery of America. ✪ Mon-Fri 10-18 h, Sat+So 10-14 h, ♦ adults € 4,50, pensioners + 65, on presentation of ID € 3,50, children under 12 free

Optionally, the signposted path behind the Columbus ship leads to the **Castillo de La Virgen [23]** and the **Plaza y Iglesia de la Encarnación [24]**. Behind the Columbus ship the way to Castillo De La Virgen is marked. After a crosswalk and over a Barranco, a natural valley bed, through which water is led into the sea during extreme rainfalls, it goes uphill to the Castillo de la Virgen. The entrance is on the left side of the building.

Plaza E Iglesia De La Encarnación: Above the pink building in which the Cabildo Insular is located, the street Cuesta La Encarnación leads to the Plaza and Iglesia De La Encarnación. The course is dominated by 10 large Indian laurel trees and offers an impressive view of the city from the sea side.

The Iglesia is on the right hand side. It is the first church built in Santa Cruz after the conquest in 1493 and the second oldest on the island around which the first houses of the emerging city were built. In 1553 it was plundered after a pirate raid, but was spared a fire. Of interest are the Flemish works of the Virgin of the Incarnation and the Archangel

Gabriel from 1522 and 1532, which, however, can only be admired during mass when the church is open.

For the rest of the tour, follow the Avenida de Las Nieves after the Columbus ship to the right in the direction of the sea and you are already on your **way back to the jetty.** Now turn right onto **Avenida Marítima.** On the right you will pass the **Castillo de Santa Catalina [25].** The fortress was a defensive station built between 1683 and 1692 after the existing structure was destroyed from the sea side by pirates. It takes its name from its proximity to the former sanctuary of Santa Catalina de Alejandria. The archway on the entrance side is decorated with the emblem of the Three Kings. The ground plan is quadrangular and has four defense towers on each corner. The Castillo is privately owned and was declared a Historical-Artistic Heritage in 1951. From here you enjoy a wonderful view of the city beach up to the offshore islands of Tenerife and La Gomera.① (front: Avenida Marítima/entrance: turn right into Calle Méndez Cabezola and then right into Calle del Catillete).

From here, on the left side, the city beach begins, the **Playa del Malecón [26].** The 550 m long and up to 120 m deep dark fine sand beach is one of the largest on the island and was filled up in 2014 for € 28 million with 700,000 cbm of sand. Thanks to the beach guard you can go swimming safely in the sea. They follow the Avenida Marítima and already see your ship from the distance.

Space for your own notes✎... ...

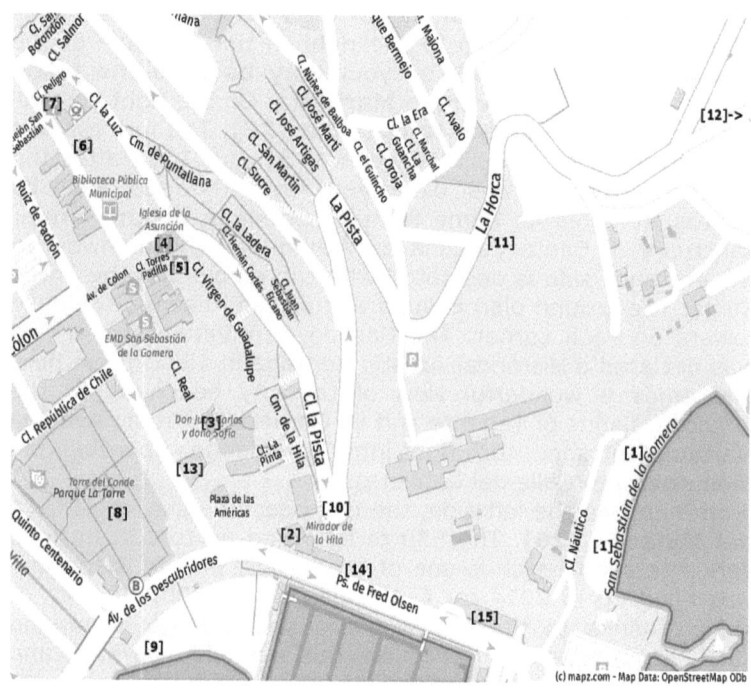

(c) mapz.com - Map Data: OpenStreetMap ODb

Space for your own notes✐... ...

19 Welcome to the capital San Sebastián de La Gomera!

They have now anchored in the harbour on the 6th largest island with 370 sqkm. La Gomera has a total population of 21,500, of whom 9,000 live in the capital.

The island was formed over 11 million years ago from the sea and, in contrast to the other Canary Islands, has not recorded any volcanic eruptions for 2 million years. Remarkable are the impressive cliffs with the fantastic rock formations. Green flowering spurge plants give the island its fresh appearance. The island became famous through Christopher Columbus, who anchored his ships on La Gomera in San Sebastián in 1492 to make all preparations for the crossing to America. After this exciting time it has become quiet around the capital.

From the cruise ship the blue line on the sidewalk and the sign Línea Azul/Blue Line - Cruceros/Cruises leads to the city centre.

On the left you will find the ferry terminal, which takes you from Tenerife to La Gomera in 50 minutes, next to the marina. At the end of the ferry terminal there is a roundabout leading to the first sights. Go straight ahead into Calle Náutico with the signposted **Playa de la Cueva beach [1]**. In this bay you will immediately come across a sundial made of concrete which shows the current time almost correctly. In front of it there are benches from which you can enjoy a fantastic view of the island of Tenerife. In bad weather Tenerife appears only in the haze, but almost always you can see the highest mountain, the Teide with 3718 m.

In the center there are 2 viewpoints on the right side. Stairs leading up to the volcanic rocks take you to platforms that once again offer a fantastic view. The second viewpoint is called Mirador de la Antorcha, on the top of which stands the sculpture of an Olympic torch. The monument commemorates the XIXth Olympic Games in 1968 in Mexico, in which a local athlete took part. The torch came from Greece to La Gomera and went on by sea to America.

The bathing bay of Playa de la Cueva is 300 m long, 60 m wide and has a black, fine sandy beach with small pebbles at the edge. The swimming is possible through an artificial breakwater, but it is an unguarded beach without a lifeguard.

On the way to the city centre you pass the small marina where you can watch the locals feed the big fish with old bread. The blue line ends at Marina La Gomera. Cross the crosswalk and turn left and you will immediately arrive at Plaza de las Américas, which becomes Plaza de la Constitución. Past the small pavilion of the tourist information you will find yourself immediately on the central The island's point of contact. On the right, flags adorn the Ayuntamiento **[2]**, the town hall of San Sebastián.

The main road where the sights are located is right next to the large ochre building. This is where **Calle Real**, the Royal Street, starts. Unfortunately, almost all the buildings, except for the churches, are closed, so that you can only understand the charm of the capital on the antique facades.

On the right side of the Plaza de la Constitución stands the **Casa de La Aduana [3]**- the customs house that served as a prison at that time.

Enjoy the flair of this beautiful street of San Sebastián with the oldest houses of the city. They date from the 18th century, are one to two storeys high and partly decorated with wooden balconies. When the city was not yet built up to the port, these balconies allowed merchants to see the arriving merchant ships in order to do business with the captains as quickly as possible before the competition.

Particularly interesting are the balconies, which are completely barred. They go back to Arab influences and enabled the ladies of the house to follow the events on the street unobserved without being seen. Note the round manhole covers embedded in the road. They remind us of the importance of the navigator Christopher Columbus for the island. In the covers a crown is enclosed, under it the 3 Columbus ships under which on a Borde "de aqui partió Colón" - "Columbus started from here", stands.

Follow Calle Real and you will see **Iglesia de La Asunción [4]** on your right. The Church of the Assumption of the Virgin Mary is the most important parish church in the capital and the most important religious building on the island. The most striking feature is the late-Gothic main portal made of red tuff stone, which was modelled on intertwined ship ropes. In 1618 the Iglesia was heavily destroyed by Berber pirates. During the reconstruction 2 side aisles were added. You should pay special attention to the interior. Impressive are the carved Mudejár wooden ceilings from Canarian pine wood, the valuable art treasures and the 10 different splendid altars. The greatest reform of the building took place in the 2nd half of the 18th century with the construction of the Capilla del Pilar chapel at the rear of the left aisle, which represents the victory of the islanders over the invaders. The large tapestry captures the fight of the Gomeros against the troops of the English admiral Charles Windham in 1743. The statue of the church's bearer of the name, the Virgen de la Asunción, stands to the left of the main altar, comes from Seville and dates back to the 18th century. ☉daily

The Archaeological Museum **Museo Arquelogico de La Gomera [5]** is located to the right of the church in the rear building complex of the row of houses and is housed in the Casa de los Echevarría. In the 18th century, the Echevarría family was one of the most influential noble families in the city, underlined by the wood-carved family coat of arms on the ochre-yellow façade. In the small renovated museum you will learn how the island was settled, how the inhabitants lived and what religious practices and symbols they used. Furthermore, an excavation site in the inner courtyard was reconstructed true to detail and a burial place was placed in a niche on the left side of the upper floor. ☉ Mo - Fr 9-14, 15-17 h, Sat + Sun closed, ✦€2,50, ➀For static reasons only 25 persons are allowed in the museum at the same time. Information folders on the exhibition will be handed out at the entrance.

Following the main street Calle Real, there is the **Casa de Colón [6]**, Christopher Columbus' house, where he had spent the night before his voyages to America. The small restored building has a small collection of clay vessels on the ground floor and temporary exhibitions on the upper floor. ☉ Mon-Fri 9 30- 13.30, 15- 17.30, ✦free admission, ⌂Calle Real, 56

Following Calle Real, you will find the small church of **Ermita de San Sebastián [7]** on the right, just after the Correos Post Office building. It dates from the 15th century and was rebuilt after repeated pirate attacks in the 16th century until it was given its present appearance in 1674. In the centre is the holy statue of the patron saint of San Sebastián, whose body is pierced by arrows. Open daily, ☉⌂ Calle Real, corner San Sebastián

Go back down Calle Real and after the parish church Iglesia de La Asunción turn right into the small Calle República de Chile. On the left you will see the **Parque de la Torre del Conde [8]**, in the centre of which stands the **Torre del Conde**- the Count's tower. It was a fortress built around 1450 and is the only existing medieval military fortress on the Canary Islands and served as a refuge for the islanders during pirate attacks. Here the Gomeros meet during the day until the late evening hours, in order to relax with child and family. To the side of the tower and distributed in the park, there are Noria water fountains, set in motion by donkeys to pump water from wells.

If you haven't noticed it yet, flame trees have been planted all over the city, and they're all around the tower. Beautiful trees, which carry ferns-leaves in the crown, bloom red in the summer and of which only brown, long pods are to be seen in the Canarian winter-months.

In the lower part of the park you now exit towards the sea, come onto the main road Avenida de los Descubridores and see the **Playa de San Sabastián [9]**. With a length of 1km it is the most beautiful beach of the island, which was also awarded with the blue flag. The black fine sandy beach has free umbrellas and is perfect for relaxing. The sea is divided by a breakwater, but the quiet and safe part of the beach is located along the promenade, at the back of the bay. From here you can also look directly at your cruise ship. Here the tour of the capital ends. The promenade takes you directly back to the ship.

You can also reach the viewpoint **Mirador de la Hila [10]**, the Gofiomühle **Molina de Gofio [11],** and the lighthouse **Faro de San Cristóbal [12]** in 40 minutes on foot and after a total of 1.7 km.

Discover beautiful views over San Sebastián and look from the plateau of the lighthouse overlooking the city to your cruise ship:

From the main street Paseo Fred Olsen, turn right into Plaza de las Americas, where you will find the Ayuntamiento Town Hall, decorated with flags, on your right. From here, follow the street called Calle Virgen de Guadalupe.

Now you go into the 2nd street before the Pizzeria Agando into the Calle de la Pinta. From here, take the uphill stairs to Calle de la Pista and follow the uphill road to the right. The Mirador de la Hila is located just before the next uphill left turn. The viewing platform offers a great view over the marina to the main beach Playa de San Sebastián. Follow the road up to the Parador de La Gomera, the only 4-star hotel on the island.

In front of the Parador, follow the road again and you will see an old mill on your right that looks like a windmill.

This is a gofio mill from 1913. The property is privately owned, so you can only take a photo. In the 19th century this type of mill was developed, which for the first time made it possible to grind the grain without having to carry it up the stairs.

The road leads past the Cementerio, the cemetery of the city. Shortly after, the road forks and you take the turn-off to the right, into the Camino del Faro. From here you can already see the red and white lighthouse.

At the former house of the lighthouse keeper stands the former small lighthouse, which was replaced in 1976 by the new, automatically operated and higher tower.

To the left of it a trail leads past the tower, which you then follow to the right to get past the old lighthouse. Shortly afterwards there is an unpaved plateau from where you can enjoy an incredible view over the coast up to the cruise ship.① As an author I would like to point out again and again that most accidents on the Canary Islands happen to careless holidaymakers. Please do not climb unsecured volcano mountains or swim on unattended beaches.

Want a little more ship?

If you feel like a boat trip to the Valle Gran Rey, where the flair of the hippie era and a touch of flower power has been preserved, you can book a ferry ticket with the Fred Olsen Express. Directly from the port in San Sebastián you reach Valle Gran Rey in 70 minutes along the steep coast, across the Playa de Santiago. Here you have the possibility to stroll through the small town, to eat or to bathe. The small dark sandy beach **Playa de Vueltas** is close to the jetty, the promenade leads you along the coast to the stone beach **Playa de La Puntilla**. The oversized bronze statue of the aboriginal Hautacuperche is enthroned here. He is still revered today by the Gomeros, because in 1488 he led the rebellion against the hated Spanish island ruler Fernán Peraza el Joven and was killed by an arrowhead of his opponents.

Tickets online at **www.fredolsen.es**

On the Spanish/English page click on Origin and Destination- La Gomera, then on Origin- Harbour **S.S. de La Gomera** and then on Destination- Harbour **Valle Gran Rey**. Online booking is cheaper than buying a ticket at the counter in the mooring terminal on the right hand side at the exit of your ship. Online price for return, at least 1 day before departure: adults 20,00 €, children from 4-11 years 12,00 €.

If you buy the tickets at the counter, the price per adult is 28.00 €, for children 16.00 €. ① **Please note that you must take your identity card or passport with you and show it.**

Departure: San Sebastián 10.15 a.m. at Valle Gran Rey 11.25 a.m.

Return journey: Valle Gran Rey 15.30 hrs to San Sebastián 16.40 hrs

<u>Finally, I would like to give you a tip for typical island delicacies and souvenirs.</u>

Delicious fresh pastries and biscuits typical of the island can be found in the **Dulcería Mendoza [13]** in the parallel street to the main street, Calle Ruiz de Padrón.

Also typical for Gomera are the **Papas locas**, French fries with mayonnaise, mustard and ketchup. The sauces are poured like a grid over the chips, which are then served pure with plucked chicken or beef.

You should also try a **Barraquito**, a layered coffee made from sweet condensed milk, espresso, milk coffee and milk foam, which is also served with liqueur. They are particularly tasty and inexpensive in **Pub El Muelle [14]**, located opposite Marina La Gomera, where the blue line for cruise ships ends, on the opposite side of the road.

The largest selection of souvenirs at the best price can be found in **Laurisilva [15]**, which is directly opposite the marina. Besides the usual souvenirs you will find clothes, bags, aloe vera products, jams, wines, jewellery, mojo sauces, cigars and much more.

20 General Information Canaries
bathing safety

- Every year people die in the Canary Islands bathing! Please note that the Atlantic Ocean is extremely dangerous in the Canary Islands. Strong currents, undercurrents and sudden waves with a strong suction effect are not uncommon. Even experienced professional swimmers have already lost their lives through carelessness. As soon as the red flag is hoisted, there is an absolute ban on swimming. Don't go in the water just because there's a few people swimming in it. If the flag is yellow, it is recommended to stay only near the beach. If you witness a bathing accident, do not swim afterwards. If available, inform the stand supervisor at the guarded beaches, otherwise call 112. You can also report the incident in English.

Banks and Money

- In all larger towns there are banks and ATMs. When withdrawing with a money card, however, sometimes high fees are incurred as everywhere abroad. It is best to have a small supply of cash with you and pay all further amounts with a credit card.

Bus / Public transport

- The public buses in the Canary Islands are called Guaguas and run regularly between all the major towns. The departure times can be found directly at the bus stops (Paradas). Bus trips are quite cheap in the Canary Islands.

Doctor and medical care

- In principle, medical care in the Canary Islands is in line with international standards, but depending on the island, it may be limited. It is advisable to take out travel sickness insurance. For invoices you may have to pay in advance, so always have a detailed invoice issued so that you can settle it later with your insurance company.

emergencies

- The general emergency number is 112 without area code! English is also spoken here. You can also contact the ship's reception directly, where the numbers of doctors, embassies, etc. are known.

Festivities and holidays

- The Canary Islands celebrate many general and island festivals. Also individual communities on each individual island have additionally still their local celebrations and holidays. The Cannario likes to celebrate. Depending on the island and the municipality, it is recommended to visit Googlen on the Internet beforehand. The festivities are often very interesting, as they are celebrated with original clothes and highly traditional.

NUDISM

- Basically, on the beaches of the Canary Islands nudism is not welcome. As always, however, there are official exceptions. On Gran Canaria the beach between Playa de Ingles and Maspalomas in the dunes is a popular nudist hiking area. Also on Lanzarote there is an official FFK area in the north, in the village Charco de Palo.

opening hours

- In the tourist areas, the shops are usually open 7 days a week from morning to evening. On the Canary Islands, however, the classic siesta still exists, so that shops have closed from 1 p.m. until 5 p.m. Since there is no shop opening hours law, you will always find a place to shop and stay.

pharmacies

- There are pharmacies in all major towns.

photography

- There are no special additional regulations, but as anywhere in the world they should not film/record police or military areas. Apart from that it is often called "fire free" when photographing.

rental cars

- On the Canary Islands rental cars are already available for a reasonable price. In every port, at the airport and also in all tourist places there are rental stations. Reservations can also be made in advance via the Internet.

Services / Fairs

- The Canarian population is mostly Catholic and there is an Emitta, church, etc. in almost every village. The opening hours are always at the church, but the Sunday service at noon is always obligatory. Since many interesting churches only open during trade fairs, it is advisable to visit a trade fair.

Shopping and business hours

- There are no fixed opening hours in the Canary Islands. In tourist areas the shops are often open from morning till evening. These shops are also open on Sundays. In normal residential areas or big cities there is often the classical lunch break between 1 p.m. and 5 p.m.

sun

- Attention. The Canary Islands are not far away from the equator, so that even in December / January UV values are reached that only occur in summer in England. Don't be fooled by the clouds in the sky. Depending on the skin type, it is recommended to use sun cream when going ashore as well as on the ship.

theft
- The crime rate in the Canary Islands is very low, but of course there are also "bad fingers" here. But please do not leave anything of value open and visible. In case of theft / crime you can call the police directly with 112. In order to be able to assert your claims against your insurance company at a later date, it is essential that you have a police record drawn up.

time lag
- The Canary Islands are located in the Western European time zone (also known as Greenwich Mean Time or GMT).

A

Alameda de Colón · 36
Aquarium Poema del
Mar · 25
Archivo Histórico
Provincial · 33
Auditorio de Tenerife ·
17, 18
Avenida del Puente · 49,
50
Ayuntamiento de Santa
Cruz de La Palma · 49

B

Balcones Tipícos · 51
Barraquito · 62
Biblioteca Insular · 35

C

Cabildo de Tenerife · 7
Calle Léon y Castillo · 22,
27, 40
Calle O´Daly · 46, 47, 48
Calle Real · 46, 48, 58, 59
Casa Amarilla · 40
Casa Consistorial · 32
Casa de Carnaval · 9, 11
Casa de Carta · 7
Casa de Colón · 33, 34, 59
Casa de La Aduana · 58
Casa de la Pólvera · 17,
19
Casa del Miedo · 9
Casa Museo Peréz
Galdos · 36

Casa Museo Unamuno ·
21
Casa Salazar · 46
Casino de Santa Cruz de
Tenerife · 13
Castillo de la Luz · 27
Castillo de La Virgen · 54
Castillo de San
Cristóbal · 6, 18
Castillo de San Juan · 17,
18
Castillo de Santa
Catalina · 55
Castillo San Gabriel · 40,
41
Catedral Basílica de
Santa Ana · 29, 32
Centro Atlántico de Arte
· 33
Centro Comercial El
Muelle · 25
Centro de Arte La
Recova · 10
Centro de
Interpretación
Bajada de la Virgen ·
47
Charco de San Ginés · 39,
41
Cien Caras del Auditorio
· 17, 18
Círculo Mercantil · 37
Convento San Pedro de
Alcantara
Franciscanos · 12
Cruz de Montañés · 7

D

Dulcería Mendoza · 62

E

Ermita de San Antonio
Abad · 34
Ermita de San
Sebastián · 59
Ermita de San Telmo · 30
Estación de Guagas · 22, 29, 30

F

Faro de San Cristóbal · 60
FEDAC · 37

G

Gabinete Literario · 35, 36
Gobierno de Canarias · 10
Gobierno Militar · 30
Gran Hotel Arrecife · 41, 42

H

Hotel AC Gran Canaria · 27

I

Iglesia de La Asunción · 58, 59
Iglesia de la
Concepción · 8, 9, 13
Iglesia de los
Franciscanos · 37
Iglesia de Salvador · 48

Iglesia de San Agustín · 31
Iglesia de San
Francisco · 12, 32, 36
Iglesia de San Ginés · 40
Isla de la Madera · 10

K

Kiosko de la Música · 30
Kiosko Modernista · 30

L

La Carabela III · 26
La Recova · 9, 49, 50
La Regenta · 27
La Tinerfeña · 7
La Vegueta · 25
Las Rotondas · 21
Laurisilva · 62
Librería del Calbildo · 37

M

Marina Lanzarote · 39, 41
Mercado de Vegueta · 29, 31
Mercado del Puerto · 27
Mercado Municipal · 22
Mirador de la Hila · 60
Molina de Gofio · 60
Monumento a los
Caídos · 7
Monumento a Santiago
García Sanabiria · 16
Museo Arquelogico de
La Gomera · 59
Museo Canario · 32
Museo de Historia · 40

Museo Diocesano de Arte Sacro · 33
Museo Educación- Germán González · 48
Museo Elder · 26
Museo Insular · 52
Museo Internacional de Arte Contemporáneo MIAC · 42
Museo Naval- Barco De La Virgen · 54

N

Nuestra Señora del Rosario · 21

P

Palacete Rodríguez Queguez · 37
Palacio de Justicia · 31
Palacio Episcopal · 33
Palmetum · 17, 19
Papas locas · 62
Paroquia de San Francisco · 52
Parque de la Torre del Conde · 59
Parque de San Telmo · 30
Parque García Sanabria · 14, 16
Parque Marítimo Manrique · 17
Parroquia San Francisco · 12
Placeta de Borrero · 51
Playa Chica · 21
Playa de la Cueva · 57
Playa de La Puntilla · 61

Playa de Las Alcaravaneras · 25
Playa de las Canteras · 26
Playa de las Teresitas · 6
Playa de Reducto · 41
Playa de San Sabastián · 60
Playa de Vueltas · 61
Playa del Malecón · 55
Plaza de España · 6, 12, 15, 18, 46, 48
Plaza de La Alameda · 54
Plaza de la Iglesia · 7, 49
Plaza de los Patos · 15
Plaza de San Antonio Abad · 34
Plaza de San Francisco · 36, 52
Plaza de Santa Ana · 32
Plaza de Vandale · 50
Plaza del Chicharro · 10
Plaza e Iglesia de Santo Domingo · 47
Plaza Principe de Asturias · 11
Plaza San Sebastián y Ermita · 48
Plaza Santo Domingo · 10
Plaza Weyler · 14, 15
Plaza y Iglesia de la Encarnación · 54
Plazuela De La Cruz Del Tecero · 53
Pub El Muelle · 62
Puente de las Bolas · 40
Puerto de Los Marmóles · 39

Q

QUÉ MUAC · 42

R

Rambla Azul · 9
Real Club Nautico · 41, 50
Reklametafeln · 10
Roloj de Flores · 16

S

Skulptur von Enrique González Bethencourt · 11

T

TEA · 8
Teatro Chico · 49
Teatro Circo de Marte · 48
Teatro Cuyas · 37
Teatro Peréz Galdos · 31
Torre del Conde · 59
Tribunal de Justicia · 12

V

Valle Gran Rey · 61, 62

FSC

www.fsc.org

MIX

Papier aus ver-
antwortungsvollen
Quellen

Paper from
responsible sources

FSC® C105338